101 AWESOME THINGS
YOU MUST DO IN

Costa Rica

James Hall

101 AWESOME THINGS YOU MUST DO IN COSTA RICA

Copyright © 2017 by JAMES HALL

All rights reserved. Printed in the United States of America. No part of this publication may be reproduced, distributed, or transmitted in any form or by any means, including photocopying, recording, or other electronic or mechanical methods, without the prior written permission of the publisher, except in the case of brief quotations embodied in critical reviews and certain other noncommercial uses permitted by copyright law.

Information contained within this book is for educational purposes only. Although the author and publisher have made every effort to ensure that the information in this book was correct at press time, the author and publisher do not assume and hereby disclaim any liability to any party for any loss, damage, or disruption caused by errors or omissions, whether such errors or omissions result from negligence, accident, or any other cause.

For information visit:

http://www.JamesHallTravel.com

ISBN-10: 1544233442
ISBN-13 : 978-1544233444

First Edition: March 2017

10 9 8 7 6 5 4 3 2 1

JAMES HALL

CONTENTS

101 AWESOME THINGS YOU MUST DO IN I

CONTENTS 3

FOREWORD: PURA VIDA PHILOSOPHY 8

CHAPTER 1: THE BASICS 17

    To-do *17*

    Parks *18*

    Diving *20*

    Ziplining *22*

CHAPTER 2: SAN JOSE 25

    1- Bienvenido el Capital de Costa Rica *25*

    2- Sampling and Snacking at Feria Verde Marcado *26*

    3- Let Me Eat Cake at Cafe Miel *27*

    4- Outdoor Patios at El Mundo *28*

    5- The Art and Leisure Section *28*

    6- Bookstores and Storytelling *29*

    7- Eat like a Local *29*

    8- Butterfly Gardens *30*

    9- Museo de Jade *31*

10-Teatro Nacional... 32

11- Café de los Deseos 33

CHAPTER 3: DAY TRIPS FROM SAN JOSE 34

12- Paramo Wildlife Refuge 34

13- La Paz Waterfalls 35

14-The Zany Topiary of Zancero 35

15- Ghost Hunting and Graffiti in Sanatorio Durán 36

16- Poas Volcano 37

17- Trails at Tapanti National Park 38

18- Lily Pads of Cachi Lake 38

19- Iglesia de Nuestra Señora de la Limpia Concepción 39

20- Iglesia de San Jose 39

21- Chirripo Mountain 40

22- La Fortuna 40

23- Arenal Volcano 41

24- Venado Caves 41

25- White Water Rafting of Rios Penas Blancas, Balsa y Toro .. 42

26- Piscina de los Pobres 43

27- Soaring above Volcanos 43

28- Viento Fresco 44

29- Llanos de Cortés 45

CHAPTER 4: MONTEVERDE AND SANTA ELENA 46

30- Treehouse Cafe 46

31- Walk through the Treetops 47

32- Climb the Giant Ficus 48

33- Hummingbird Gardens 48

34- Coffee Plantations and Tastings 50

35- Aerial Tram 52

CHAPTER 5: SAN GERARDO DE DOTA 53

- 36- Breathing in a Cloud 53
- 37- Quetzales National Park 54

CHAPTER 6: TORTUGUERO 56

- 38- Sea Turtle Mothers, Hatchlings, and Running to Freedom .. 57
- 39- Learn More about Turtles 59
- 40- Glide Through Central America's Amazon 59
- 41- Paddle Your Own Canoe 61
- 42- Night Tours 61
- 43- Hiking Tortuguero Hill 62
- 44- Be Amongst the Treetops 63
- 45- Sport Fishing 63
- 46- Birdwatching 64

CHAPTER 7: LIMON 66

- 47- Lounging in Limon 66
- 48- Oxtail 67
- 49- Get Down with Rastafarian Beats, Spanish Pop or Swinging Salsa 68
- 50- Playa Bonita 68
- 51- Dia de Las Culturas 69
- 52- Festival of Flowers 69
- 53- Eating Authentically at Miss Edith's 71
- 54- Dance with Chiquita Bananas 71
- 55- Reserva Biológica Hitoy Cerere 72

CHAPTER 8: PUERTO VIEJO 73

- 56- Caribbean Pura Vida 73
- 57- Arise with the Madrugar 75
- 58- Coffee, Java & Chocolate 76
- 59- Biking 77
- 60- Surf the Salsa Brava 80

61- Hangout with the Cast of the Little Mermaid 81
62- Petting Jungle Kitties 82
63- Chocolate Forests 83
64- Drinks and Dancing 84
Conclusion to Caribbean Coast 85

CHAPTER 9: PACIFICO NORTE 86

65- El Museo de Sabanero 88
66- Cowboy for a Day 88
67- Nature's Spa Day at Rincon de la Vieja Volcan 89
68- Walking on the Battlefields of Santa Rosa National Park ... 92
69- Paddle Along in Palo Verde National Park 93
70- Cave Diving in Barra Honda National Park......................... 94
71- Sea Caves of Playa Ventanas... 95
72- Dead Men Tell No Tails on Bahia de los Piratas 96

CHAPTER 10: DIVING IN GUANACASTE 97

73- Octopus Hunting off the Catalina Islands............................ 97
74- The Rainbow Fish off the Gulf 98
75- Noshing at the Farmers Market 99
76- Turtle Tours at Playa Grande 100
77- Surfing the Big Surf... 102

CHAPTER 11: PENÍNSULA DE NICOYA 104

78- Surfing and Seclusion of Mal País & Santa Teresa 104
79- Cabo Blanco National Park.. 105
80- Horseback Riding to the Hidden Cascades of El Chorro..... 106
81- Ghost Hunting on Cabuya Island 107
82- Casting Spells in a Bioluminescence Tour........................... 109
83- The Hidden Black Sand Beach of Playa Zancudo 111
84- Tarcoles River Boat Crocodile Tour..................................... 112

CHAPTER 12: JACO 113

85- Hablando Espanol *114*

86- Hablando Espanol con Ballar *115*

87- Jaco Canopy Zipline Tour *115*

88- Jaco Rainforest Aerial Tram *116*

89- Scarlet Macaws in Carara National Park........................... *116*

90- Silence in Manuel Antonio... *117*

91- Canopy Safari Zip Line *119*

92- White Water Rafting down Naranjo River *120*

CHAPTER 13: UVITA **122**

93- Become Clean in Cascada Verde *122*

94- Walk the Whale's Tail at Marino Ballena National Park... *123*

CHAPTER 14: DOMINICAL **125**

95- Flying and Paragliding... *125*

96- Poisonous Frogs in Parque Reptilandia *126*

97- Ojochal: The Gateway to Osa Peninsula *128*

CHAPTER 15: CAÑO ISLAND **130**

98- Diving in the Devil's Rock *131*

99- Shark Tank.. *131*

100- The Coral Gardens *132*

101- Mysterious Spheres of Caño Island *132*

FINAL WORDS **135**

BONUS: THE SECRET FOR CHEAP FLIGHTS **137**

1. Look for Error Fares *138*

2. Use Throwaway Tickets *138*

3. The Secret to book $1,000 flights for just $20 or less. (MOST IMPORANT) *139*

Foreword: Pura Vida Philosophy

Bienvenido de 101 Adventures in Costa Rica! I'm sure your reasons for traveling to Costa Rica vary from those of the person sitting next to you on the plane. Maybe you wanted the thrill of zip lining while they just wanted a quiet place catch up on the new Fifty Shades of Grey book. Maybe you want to improve your Spanish while they want to improve their tan. Whatever the reasons for visiting the happiest country in the world, you will never be disappointed with this idyllic destination.

I'm going to take you on a tour of the world's happiest country and tailor the trip to your timeframe and desires. Let me start with some background on my own experiences. I wanted to travel to Costa Rica because it sounded colorful. It sounded like a place with vibrancy, and I was aching to escape into a neon painted world, away from the gray concrete New York winter I was living in at the time. I wanted green and growth. I desired the sound of birds telling me the day has begun, not the ever-present sirens and clunking rumble of the trash trucks, I was tired of the endless bustle of the city, the brisk walks to the subway, a place that turns too cold and too busy to enjoy being alive. I was looking for the opposite—I wanted to replace the concrete jungle with the real thing, a land that doesn't deny me warmth for half of the year. Most importantly, my body had forgotten what it was like to breathe—which is a totally weird thing to say. Not in the literal 'my face is turning blue,' but I was breathing only because it was necessary, not because I was pausing and taking in the ephemeral moment.

Breathing is a small, but vital, act that is often forgotten. I was surviving in New York, but I wasn't living. I had an intense and irresistible desire for freedom.

Once I arrived in Costa Rica, every morning I was awakened by my joy. I was existing in a land that was more green than gray, more grass than streets, more music than alarms. Costa Rica is dripping with flora and fauna; it literally creeps and grows into your kitchen, wraps itself around your table and even sneaks its way into your closets. I saw colors so vibrant I thought only machines could make them. There were birds, flowers, and fish as colorfully decorated as Lisa Franks prismatic stencil sets (or ….that not even Lisa Franks wildest acid trip could create). I honestly couldn't believe they were natural.

Costa Rica is an omnipresent wilderness; and you can't help but get tangled up in it. The locals recognize the blessing of living in one of the most biodiverse areas in the world and understand the importance of taking care of their land. They don't take the richness they enjoy for granted and go to great lengths to maintain it. These ties to nature have also shaped the philosophy of their country—Pura Vida. Pure life—a life unconstrained by technology, balanced by nature and composed of tranquility. It is about taking care of the important aspects of life: relationships, personal wellbeing and the earth.

This philosophy is probably why Costa Rica has achieved the title as the **#1 happiest country in the world**, ranking as the highest population with satisfied and active social lives, low stress levels and low ecological footprints. The locals, known by the nickname 'Ticos,' have created the perfect combination of enriching their environment, cultivating deep friendships and family relationships, and maintaining low stress levels. (When will they bottle this and sell it at CVS pharmacies?!). All of these aspects are woven together to create a blanket of the perfect pura vida life. Those who live closer to nature and value human connections over money tend to have fewer instances of stress related problems and handle stress differently. Ticos are known for having longer lives and claim to have more mental peace. Achieving pura vida seems to be a surrendering to the universe and appreciating what you have in the present moment.

Few countries claim to live by such a simple philosophy that isn't wrapped up in pride, ambition, or arrogance. It isn't a philosophy that is preached but not practiced. Unlike other nations in the world, Ticos have implemented political policies for the protection and preservation of their opulent landscape. They understand that economic health and healthy ecosystems are incredibly linked, for example, almost all electricity comes from natural and local sources.

These policies have helped give Costa Rica the prestige of being one of the largest ecotourism countries in the world.

The preservation and peace of their country is such a priority they even dismantled their army in 1948. President José Figueres Ferrer abolished the military and turned Costa Rica into a pacifist state after victory in the civil war. "Blessed is the Costa Rican mother who knows that her son at birth will never be a soldier," has become another motto for Ticos. This quote given by Ryoichi Sasakawa, a Japanese politician and philanthropist, during a visit to Costa Rica after the eradication of the military.

The deconstruction of the army was replaced by universal health care and education. It is a country that has put the health and wellbeing of its people at the same level of importance as the environment, and one can easily say that Costa Rica takes care. Ticos recognize that humans do not dominate nature, but are part of a symbiotic system that we were born into, and that other countries have decided to evolve out of. They take care of what will affect the community, putting family, the environment and their enjoyment of life as a priority for the country.

There are several cultural cues that illuminate what a country represents and values, one being the images and symbols on their currency. In America we have all of our past presidents sternly facing each other in your wallet; in Mexico there are revolutionaries and artists proudly staring back at you as you purchase your chocolate caliente, and in Costa Rica there are sloths....and monkeys.....and sharks on their money. A colorful zoo weighs down your pockets.

Look at what Costa Rica has accomplished by eradicating the military, investing in health and education instead, and fiercely implementing protection of the environment. Holding the record for hosting the most biodiverse area in the world, and earning global acclaim for being the happiest country in the world. HOW CAN YOU NOT WANT TO BE HERE? Damn Costa Rica, you fine!

Now, before I traveled to Costa Rica, I couldn't help but roll my eyes when my Brooklyn yoga teacher would be in a headstand and pontificate about "finding herself while canopy walking in Monteverde," with her long blonde hair cascading onto the ground like the waterfalls in La Paz. They actively live out the values that blonde yoga teachers from Brooklyn pontificate about—"finding herself" while hiking Arenal by La Fortuna. But I'm not going to lie, as a New Yorker with a mild skepticism to most things crunchy granola—who ran away to Costa Rica to escape winter—I was taken aback by the omnipresence of the pura vida philosophy. Like a spider web, pura vida is this invisible nexus that connects everyone to each other and the planet—a symbiotic relationship that is maintained both by its people and land. The land gives to the people and the people give back.

Pura vida is more than a philosophy, it is a symbiotic sustaining life force. It is not only for the locals, anyone who breaths the air can experience pura vida. It is part of the biospheric respiratory system, an exchange of breath between all organisms. Like air, pura vida is released from the diverse flora and inhaled by all. Once inhaled, it is filtered, absorbed and flows through the heart to every tiny capillary, circulating from our toes to our mind. After reinvigorating the body, it is released back for the forests to absorb and continue the cycle. It is never seen, but its presence is always felt. Personally, Costa Rica taught me how to really breath—which totally sounds weird—but once there I wasn't gasping for air like in New York where you sometimes forget, or holding my breath to avoid the stench of the subway, but actually breathing in the way our lungs were intended to function.

I don't want to just tell you about it; I want to show you. I want to take you through the wild jungles to find a piece of yourself you have never known was missing. An ancestral perspective our modern world has domesticated. To wander the way our ancestors did in the ever present moment. There is no past or future in Costa Rica, only the pura vida present.

Costa Rica contains multitudes: simultaneously lava and waves; relaxing and adventurous; edgy and peaceful; mysterious and honest. It is a place where every day is an opportunity to experiment with life, and a chance to be alive and shout 'Aprovecho!' (I seize the day).

This book is a guide on how to achieve pura vida, because regardless of why you think you are going, pura vida is what you are seeking. There is no limit to it, the only limits are within yourself. This is not a road, but an unmarked trail with breadcrumbs left for you to follow if you choose, but I suggest you make your own path. I am giving you a mere 101 suggestions, but the opportunities truly are endless. Whatever your reason for choosing Costa Rica, be it to escape the winter, to feel your heart pulse to a jungle rhythm, or to enjoy quiet nights on a beach warmed by a bonfire and a blanket of stars—the infectious spirit of pura vida will have you reconsidering that return flight home.

Welcome to the land of pour over coffee, open air architecture, and sloths, all here to help you to find your breath again.

Chapter 1: The Basics

Let's start with the basics...

To-do

Costa Rica truly is a land of adventure. It is like flying into the first scene of Jurassic Park (oh yeah, it was filmed here). Let's begin with discussing the 'endless activities;' I hate the cliché's but seriously, there is so much to do here. It's not like you're visiting Iceland in the wintertime and each of their 'endless activities' is just a different brand of beer). Most of the time in Costa Rica you can do the same activities in different geographic areas, so if you only have time to visit the Pacific side and want to go ziplining, horseback riding and surfing you can. I will list the best places to do those activities throughout the whole country.

Parks

It is easy to assume that most individuals interested in visiting Costa Rica are here in large part for the nature. That may even be a ridiculous understatement. It is the kind of beauty that, fills the landscape before you, even when you close your laptop and your desktop background or screensaver goes away, the beautiful scenery is there before you... and it is real. Scenery so idyllic it is no small wonder that the humans who roam this land are some of the happiest in the world. It is easy to oversimplify and think that since nature plays such a dominant role in Costa Rican culture, economics and lifestyle, that the country is just one great big park—and you wouldn't be wrong. But like I stated earlier, Costa Rica's nature contains multitudes, it is unpredictable and the experience is ineffable.

Costa Rica is a little slice of earth that contains so much, perhaps making up for Antarctica which—lets be real here—takes up so much space and gives back basically nothing else but penguins. (No hate intended guys, hey penguins gotta be somewhere!) Once I was walking along a mangrove in Uvita, headed towards a rock mass shaped like a giant whale's tail, and found a tree that I appropriately taxonomize as a 'Gobstopper Tree'—the bark was actually shades of green, purple and orange. As you peeled back a layer, beneath it would be a layer of orange, then peel back another layer to find purple, and then green, in this repetitive secondary color wheel cycle.

Costa Rica's wide spectrum of ecosystems is shaped by the varying topography working within the dynamic atmospheric conditions caused by the oceans that surround the country, and is able to parent several different types of biomes—coexisting side by side. It's like the wonder mother who has given birth to too many children with different personalities yet manages to satisfy them all. From mangroves to cloud forests, and coral reefs to paramos, what else could you ask for!

Now, the interesting thing about Costa Rican activities is that although they may seem completely opposite from each other—ziplining to diving to canopy walking to surfing—they are all centered around controlling one thing: your breath. Without it, these can become the most horrifying experience, but with full control of your breathing these adventure activities become consciousness raising experiences. The beauty of Costa Rican activities is they actually do take you out of your element and thrust you into something new—being flown hundreds of feet in the air, exploring the immeasurable depths of the ocean, or walking among the tops of the trees.

Land gives us a false sense of security about our mortality. We take for granted that most of us will not suddenly die of disease, kidnapping or revenge like our ancestors did. Yet, activities like ziplining or diving, force us to recognize the precariousness of our mortality when our two legs are not firmly on land. Although both activities are about experiencing our bodies in different elements—wind and water—they both evoke the same thoughts. And give you great views that you would never have experienced had you not submerged yourself into a different element.

Diving

Diving can feel chaotic because you are forced to trust an oxygen tank. So, you focus on your breathing and practice the exaggerated inhalations to build your trust. Drowning is a horrible way to go. On land, we barely recognize when we are breathing, yet with diving it is the only thing that keeps you sane. If you begin to panic all hell breaks loose. The external lungs attached to your back make you intensely focused on your breath and require you to immerse yourself in the moment. Once you become acclimated to breathing underwater—what feels so unnatural to our bodies and that our minds try to reject—the real magic of the life aquatic begins. Underwater, time drips by as you float along with bypassing sea turtles, barracudas, or sea cucumbers just getting on with their day. The warmth of the water blankets you from sound and puts you under a spell, causing you to forget how long you have been there. The concept of time is lost and no longer relevant. You are too engrossed with finding octopus, petting starfish or breaking up schools of fish. It is so interesting to think that they don't know what a day is, they are always in the present moment and focused on the present task. No cares or worries of whether there will be food tomorrow or if the cute sea turtle likes them back, they weightlessly glide to the next sea snail or reef. The longer you're down there, your body softens, relaxes, and slowly dances around in an underwater elegance. The water feels endless filled with a peaceful complexity.

It isn't until your slow ascent back towards the sun, and after your head pops up from underwater that you realize you have been gone for an hour. "WHAT?! I have been looking for octopus for an hour? But I was gone only 5 minutes?!" Diving is like stepping into the wardrobe to Narnia, years pass in minutes. Underwater, you have all the time in the world, because there is no time. I think I cried the first time I tried scuba diving—it was the most peaceful thing I had experienced at the time. I always long to go back and live out my mermaid fantasies.

Ziplining

Want a taste of such adventure, but have an aversion to getting your hair wet? If all that serenity of the ocean and being underwater doesn't entice you, then maybe ziplining could be the activity for you.

Ziplining pulls from the opposite adventure spectrum. Ziplining gives you the adrenaline rush of a coffee high that doesn't go away for days. You don't have time to think before you are pushed into thin air. Feeling hands actively push you away from solid ground is the most un-nurturing feeling, but you don't have time to wallow in your abandonment because you are 50, 100, or 1000 meters off the ground. You are screaming and soaring from such great heights. Then you realize that Rachel McAdams probably didn't know what the hell she was talking about in the movie *The Notbook* regarding wanting to be a bird because this is GODDAMN TERRIFYING!

Your body is a bit more reactionary to being out of its comfort zone this time, which is understandable. It is hard to turn off the survival instinct thoughts of "I'M GOING TO DIE" or "I AM FALLING!" when the only thing keeping you uplifted as you are propelled over the jungle is a smallish circular piece of metal. Again, only once you remember to breathe can the thrill turn from chaos to insane awareness. Remembering to breathe allows you to be in and enjoy the moment, allowing you to realize the true rarity and beauty of the moment. You see everything at once— like how the landscape is interconnected and molded over centuries of evolution, growth and destruction. The world feels expansive and open, until a good guide gently grabs hold of your speeding body and grounds you safely back onto earth. It was far better than any dress I have ever bought.

The reason I recommend doing both activities is

because they both achieve the same goal—maintaining your breathing and being completely submerged in the moment. Joy is achieved from both, a beautiful discovery of you and your limits. Can you handle greater heights or deeper depths? How much further can you expand yourself in our ever growing universe?

Chapter 2: San Jose

1- Bienvenido el Capital de Costa Rica

If you are heading straight for the hills you will most likely fly into San Jose. To be honest, San Jose is an unavoidable eyesore if you plan on exploring a lot of Costa Rica. It is plopped right in the middle of the country and it is typically necessary to go through it if you want to travel coast to coast. It is small, polluted, and has some areas that are less than pleasant to walk in. As a solo traveler, it was one of the few places I sometimes didn't feel comfortable in during the day or night. HOWEVER, that is not to say I didn't find some gems while living there. If you are unlucky enough to have to spend a night—here are the areas that make up for it.

2- Sampling and Snacking at Feria Verde Marcado

Feria Verde Marcado: This market is a bohemian expats wet dream and is way more than just a farmers market. The Feria Verde is held every Saturday in the Aranjuez neighborhood. Going on 10 years, it's one of the first organic and gourmet markets in the country. I would walk there on Saturdays from my hostel to its home in a hidden corner of the city. Pacing down the winding hill, sheathed with wildflowers, the road opens up to an overhead view of all the heads of vendors and shoppers bobbing back and forth from booth to booth.

I love a good farmers market and this one is spectacular. As you weave back and forth between samples of guava jam, chia granola, and goat cheese you will see a mix of locals and expats enjoying the tropical bounty of Costa Rican produce and products. This tends to be a younger crowd with lots of children, so be careful when you go to sample a piece of mangostean a little hand doesn't snag it first. Most of these products are not available in Costa Rican grocery stores, so better get 'em while the gettin' is good. It is filled with not only an amazing arrangement of local fresh fruits, vegetables and Costa Rican edibles, but also incorporates a lot of meal and coffee stands, plus local artisan stalls selling clothing, jewelry, and crafts, all done by local artists. Meanwhile, local musicians play at the nexus of the market. Be still my hipster heart, there are also yoga classes in the early morning.

3- Let Me Eat Cake at Cafe Miel

After a morning so enriching in food and sound, let's go get some local coffee and snacks. Bless my baking heart—Cafe Miel. I still dream of your food porn coffee and dessert drinks, waking up to drool on my pillow and a bed littered with empty candy wrappers. This tiny cafe is the most Instagramable cafe I have visited in all of Costa Rica. Run by tattooed millennial Ticos who are too cool to make small talk with you, and desserts that make diabetes seem a little too easy, this is where the youth go to for complacer and tranquillo. Their dessert coffees make Starbucks frappacinos taste like chemical slushies. If you can snag a table in their tiny nook of a coffee shop, order the Happy Ending (a hazelnut cappuccino with a dollop of Nutella topped with a foot of whipped cream) and a Maracuja cupcake. It's enough sugar to give a small rhino diabetes, but hey—vacation calories don't count right?!

4- Outdoor Patios at El Mundo

If you are still hungry and want a taste of the finer life, visit El Mundo right next door to Cafe Miel. Providing more an Italian flair in food and aesthetic, it is a beautiful place in which to pretend you are in colonial Spain with the sounds of a Spanish guitar reverberating off of the decorative walls covered in murals vibrantly painted with giant flowers. It is a place you can indulge in being a little bougie and still not give up too much sloth money. Their drinks are better than their food. Enjoy the outdoor patio shaded by trees with an elevated view of the graffiti covered buildings.

5- The Art and Leisure Section

Now to walk off all that cake and dessert. There are great shops for a stroll around town trying to figure out what to bring back. For local or regional crafts, check out Mercado Artesanal. It is covered top to bottom with jewelry, oddities and clothing, and is kind of like walking through a hoarder's home... a hoarder who has good taste. For the sister of yours that

Instagrams every outfit, Tienda jewelry is inspired by the local resources of emeralds, gold, crystals and vibrant colors of the rainforests and coral reefs. For local prints and amazing postcards to send to your aunt who makes inappropriate Facbook comments, support Holalola. They make adorable illustrations of Costa Rican towns and areas.

6- Bookstores and Storytelling

For the inner polyglot visit Mora Books. If you want to find books in English, French or have a strange inclination to start learning German while lounging on the Costa Rican beaches, Mora books is there for you. Personally, I get really overwhelmed whenever I go into a bookstore (HAY MUCHO LEER Y NO MUCHO TIEMPO) what the Costa Ricans call aturdido, and this one especially gives you the strange wistful feeling good used bookstores should, you are surrounded by so many secrets, heartbreaks, wars and philosophies. Just hope that a stack doesn't fall on you as you purchase your Spanish version of *100 Years of Solitude*.

7- Eat like a Local

For dinner, head over to Mercado Central where

you can get a cheap but genuine Tico meal, or local ingredients to experiment with to make your own homemade meal. It is an expansive market abundant with the items every hungry Tico desires. It isn't as picturesque as the open air Mexican markets, but you will find plenty of regional Costa Rican edibles to snack and sample on. Besides the usual fresh produce, meats, and fish, there are also booths with medicinal herbs, small eateries with traditional styles, and good prices on souvenir items. Here you will be able to see that a pound of coffee beans costs about $1. DID YOU READ WHAT I JUST WROTE? $1 per pound for of some of the world's BEST COFFEE. The market spills outside to Costa Rican food trucks and carts, perfuming the streets with smells of chicken, fish, rice and beans. Careful, you have to walk through the obstacle course of Second avenida.

8- Butterfly Gardens

Stepping off the lively streets of San Jose, the Spirogyra Butterfly Garden is a serene break from the city noise. The butterflies silently drift around, some of them with patterns so intense it looks like the ceiling is filled of floating pairs of eyes staring right back at you. Watching a bright blue butterfly silently reach a plate of juicy mangos reminds you how to pause and breath again. It is a peaceful escape from the chaos and cars of San Jose, and serves to remind you why you came to Costa Rica in the first place.

9- Museo de Jade

Jade was a sacred stone for the indigenous people who ruled the land thousands of years before Columbus came knocking. The natives decorated their bodies with jade, turning it into beads, masks, ritualistic pieces and pendants carved as animals or humans. It symbolized status and power. Jade was thought to grant access to the spiritual side of world, used for a protective talisman from spirits, to access spirits through dreams and to grant a peaceful transition to the underworld. It is often known today as the 'Dream Stone,' and also holds healing powers. El Museo de Jade is home to the largest collection in the world of pre-Columbian artifacts decorated with this semi-precious stone. The collection dates the jade artifacts between 500 B.C.

-800 A.D. The wall to wall displays exhibit the auspicious success these ancient indigenous people had in carving one of the very toughest stones into jungle figures (there is even a vase that is decorated with jade and human teeth!).

10-Teatro Nacional

The National Theatre is thought of one of the finest historical buildings in San Jose with its ornate neoclassical architecture. If you have traveled to Europe, it gives you the faint reminder of the rococo buildings and designs with its colonial Spanish influence. If you are sick of salsa dancing and are craving a night of classical music for an evening, I would suggest a concert at the Teatro Nacional. You will enjoy a classical performance of the high quality you would expect to see in Vienna or Prague. The theater has a rotation of Costa Rican and foreign composers and is frequented by the National Symphonic Orchestra (NSO) which is part of Teatro Nacionale regular season.

Once inside the building you will have to admire the Alegoría al café y el banano, the theater's most infamous painting. The painting was created in Italy and shipped to Costa Rica for installation in the theater. You know those times when you can see that someone has a firm opinion about something that they clearly have no idea about? This is that kind of this painting. It is evident that the artist has probably never been to Costa Rica, let alone a banana plantation, due to the way the center figure is awkwardly handling a bunch of bananas. Real harvesters schlep them over their shoulders, not hold them from the bottom. To add insult to injury, the painting was reproduced on the old ₡5 note. So check it out to experience some colonial ignorance!

11- Café de los Deseos

The creative café, also run by hipster Ticos with tattoos of sloths in Barrio Aranjuez serves up its café frio in a tall glass with chocolate and whipped cream. Take a seat with one of these, relax, and gawk at all the hipster Ticos. Have one more coffee break before we cut loose from San Jose.

Chapter 3: Day Trips from San Jose

12- Paramo Wildlife Refuge

Take the day away from San Jose and walk. This ecosystem is what you would expect to find in the Andes of South America vs. the midpoint of tropical Central America, making it a unique adventure (and trust me, you will get plenty of beaches and tropics later). So enjoy the rarity of this land with its mountainous flora and fauna. The make-up of the forests is more of oak and elm than palm and coconut trees.

Keep your eyes peeled for tapirs, peccaries, squirrels, goats, coyotes, porcupines, armadillos, partridges, raccoons, weasels, jaguarundis, margays, foxes, pigeons and a wide range of snakes like the side-striped palm-pitviper, the fer-de-lance and the Costa Rican coral snake.

13- La Paz Waterfalls

La Paz is a great adventure away from San Jose and provides a taste of the Costa Rica you were anticipating. The self-guided tours and walking paths allow you to observe and enjoy the five waterfalls in the area. The hike should take no more than two hours. However, if you have come all the way out to La Paz, you might as well enjoy all that it offers, which is much more than just the stunning waterfall display.

Make an entire day of it and take time to explore all of the nature and animal exhibits offered, though it seems like there is an exhibit for every different type of animal and creature, including an aviary, hummingbird garden, butterfly observatory, serpentarium, jungle cats exhibit, frog exhibit, tica house and trout lake.

14-The Zany Topiary of Zancero

A bus from San Jose will take you up the windy uphill drives through the mountains of valle centro to

Zancero, the little town built on a hill. The bus will drop you off right in front of Parque Francisco Alvarado, a magical topiary filled with a zoo of bizarrely trimmed hedges.

The visionary, Evangelisto Blanco, wanted to turn the gardens into a visual amusement park, and absolutely achieved that goal. Stroll under the arches and try to guess what each hedge is trying to represent. Honestly, some of them are quite strange looking and hard to guess what the artistic intention may have been.

15- Ghost Hunting and Graffiti in Sanatorio Durán

Sanatorio Durán was created by a late president whose daughter fell ill. At the height of it, the sanitarium helped over 300 patients, until modern advancements replaced the need for the space. The building still harbors energy from the years of children facing untimely deaths. Since the last patient left, the building has only been attended by local graffiti artists who have reclaimed it, adorning the old sanitarium with giant murals in the name of art and life. Rumors still spread from visitors who say that they have heard shoes walking in the abandoned hallways, seen handprints left on glass, and witnessed flashes of childlike phantoms in the rooms as well as that of a famous nun who used to care for the bedridden children. This is definitely an alternative experience, in sharp contrast to the traditional monkeys and churches one envisions Costa Rica to be filled with. So, if you are so inclined, most definitely take advantage of this spooky modern ruin.

16- Poas Volcano

While staying in Cartago, venture out to Poas volcano, a stunning expression of the earth. Poas is an active stratovolcano—meaning it is formed by several layers upon layers of hardened lava, tephra, pumice, and volcanic ash. It is identified by a sloping profile and occasional explosive eruptions. This is still an active volcano but hasn't done any dancing since 1954. Poas contains two large crater lakes located close to the summit, Laguna Caliente and Lake Botos.

Laguna Caliente is one of the world's most acidic lakes and is unable to sustain aquatic life due to the layer of sulfur glazing the bottom of the lake. Lake Botos, on the other hand, fills an extinct crater at the end of one trail, and is extremely hospitable to many types of life forms. This crystal clear blue lake is home to numerous species of Costa Rican birds, including hummingbirds, tanagers, flycatchers, toucanets, clay-colored robins, and the quetzal. Both lakes are worth the long day's hike up to the summit.

17- Trails at Tapanti National Park

Rainforest and pre-montane rainforest make up the park with a plethora of diverse wildlife for you to get acquainted with while exploring the well-traveled paths. Several trails will lead you to expansive views of waterfalls. The land is developed enough to provide picnic areas, restaurants, bathrooms and places to barbecue your own meals.

18- Lily Pads of Cachi Lake

The spacious Cachi Lake is a great place to take your painting materials out and try to replicate the scenery. Covered with lily pads and birds scooping up their lunch, one would think if Claude Monet ever visited he would be out here painting all day. The lake isn't used for swimming, but a nearby restaurant does allow you to catch your own fish, typically trout, and will serve it hot and ready for you to eat!

19- Iglesia de Nuestra Señora de la Limpia Concepción

Unlike its brothers to the North: Mexico and Guatemala, not many ruins are present in Costa Rica. Ujarrás does hold the ruins of one of the ancient churches, Iglesia de Nuestra Señora de la Limpia Concepción. It was built in the 1580s during early colonial times, and several legends surround it regarding premonitions of the Virgin Mary, and the church was said to be constructed in honor of these stories. Regardless of why it was built, is a great peek into the earlier times of colonial Costa Rica.

20- Iglesia de San Jose

Iglesia de San Jose is the oldest church still operating in Costa Rica. Walk around one of the archaic buildings and architectural feats of Costa Rica, adorned with Spanish Colonial artifacts and religious art. Outside, expect to see several Senoras peddling local delights. Munch on an arepa or elote as you sit on the steps of the church, admiring the river and gardens that surround the church.

21- Chirripo Mountain

Chirripo Mountain is the highest peak in the whole country, a staggering 12,533 feet above sea level. The mountain is the focal point out of the expansive Chirripo National Park. The park hosts several different high-altitude microclimates: mountain paramo, lush forests, marshlands and fern groves.

There are a number of different types of treks to take depending on how long you want to be traveling. These vary from a single afternoon to an extensive three day trek up to the summit. If you have the leg strength and overall stamina. For a true gem of an experience wake up at the crack of dawn for the early morning hike to enjoy the sunrise out on the mountain range. I am never one to advocate for waking up early, but this is totally worth it. Then start your day with a wonderful pour over coffee!

22- La Fortuna

La Fortuna has a bounty of activities for any adventure you are craving. From chocolate tours to wildlife refuges, mineral hot springs to underground cave explorations, white water rafting to gentle aerial trams, La Fortuna is a place you could plan to go for a weekend and never come back. Don't worry, plenty of people are lost in the woods every year, so it is a good place to retreat into the stress-free pura vida woods and hope to never be found...

23- Arenal Volcano

Arenal is easily the most impressive volcano of Costa Rica. Standing at a lofty 5,358 feet high, this giant pyramid is the area's centerpiece and can be seen from miles away, making a nice background for the towns of La Fortuna and El Castillo. Nevertheless, I suggest you get a closer look. There are plenty of hiking trails and horseback riding tours that will have you circling around Mother Nature's opening to the underworld.

24- Venado Caves

Although everyone is at La Fortuna for the outdoor adventures, the area also has hidden secrets buried beneath the undergrowth. A subterranean land filled with stalactites, stalagmites, deep caverns, cascading rivers, ancient fossils, and a wide variety of covert critters.

These limestone caves are the outcome of tectonic shifting and a strong subterranean river, shaped and molded some 15-20 million years ago. The caves were found by the indigenous Guatuzos tribe and host tours everyday where you can walk on top of the upper crust of the underworld.

25- White Water Rafting of Rios Penas Blancas, Balsa y Toro

Costa Rica adventures are like Goldilocks and the three bears-there are enough options operating at different velocities surrounding Arenal, giving you the option to find the one that is juuuuuust right: Peñas Blancas, Balsa and Rio Toro.

The Peñas Blancas River is the easier ride, with a slow and steady current that allows you to take in the sights and wildlife living around it. The Balsa River is a little more intense and has class II and III rapids. Still nothing insanely adventurous, this ride oscillates between meditative stretches and quick twists and turns. It is enough to get your heart pumping but is still suitable for all ages. Lastly is the Toro River that makes its way from the central highlands of the Poás Volcano to the Caribbean Sea. It ventures through dense forests, deep canyons, and rolling hillsides, making it the most audacious ride out of the three and is well suited for the intrepid rafters. It is said to be a trip even for the most experienced of rafters.

26- Piscina de los Pobres

Piscina de los Pobres (Pool of the Poor) is the merging of two thermal rivers, forming a natural hot springs. Free and open to the public (even though it is generally a well-kept secret from the tourists), these mineral waters are ideal to nourish your skin and loosen your muscles after the trek to get in. This is a must if you are in the area for a while.

27- Soaring above Volcanos

I didn't grow up around volcanos, so I find them to be completely fascinating, a portal to the fiery world beneath us. When I am around them, I take advantage of being able to experience them from every perspective I can. I suggest taking the aerial tram, which provides una Buena Vista. The ethereal vantage point allows you to encompass the full magnitude of the volcano, which used to be one of the world's most active, ending in 2010. Relax as you observe this smoky mountain in the midst of the rainy forest, from the comforts of a sky tram—no physical or mental energy required.

Good for—hot springs, aerial trams, volcanos, hikes, horseback riding, ziplining, canopy tours.

28- Viento Fresco

The trip to Monteverde from La Fortuna doesn't offer much, but fortunately Viento Fresco waterfall is the midpoint between these two destinations. The hike will bring you to a series of waterfalls in the area: Serina River Waterfall, Slide Waterfall, Rainbow Waterfall, and Hidden Waterfall. The hike to the falls is the perfect way to stretch your legs after driving in your car for a few hours. If you continue the hike it will bring you to a lookout, perched above the treetops, where you can see a vast amount of land and one of the waterfalls from a distance trickling into the mountaintop. With some forethought, you can do the whole trek on horseback. Good for car ride stretches, waterfalls, hiking, horseback riding

29- Llanos de Cortés

Llanos de Cortes is the iconic waterfall filmed in any tropical movie and is just as dramatic as the actors who perform around it. You'll be able to hear its rumblings from a distance. You will trek down a steep trail to meet a 12m-high, 15m-wide waterfall. The waterfall cascades into a serine aquamarine pond laced with white sandy beaches like trim on a blue sweater. Either lay out on the beach or venture 'behind the curtains' and venture behind the waterfall to sprawl out onto the large boulders hidden on the other side. Make sure to bring your own snacks because other than foraging for your own food (which I don't suggest) there is only an occasional vendor peddling fruit or ceviche.

Chapter 4: Monteverde and Santa Elena

Elevated on the spine of Costa Rica, Monteverde is perched high above the coastal towns (so high up you can even see the coast located miles away on the bus ride to the apex of Monteverde). The town of Santa Elena, is the gateway to what is possibly the most famous cloud forest. This area is ripe with plenty of adventures, from coffee plantations, hummingbird gardens, giant ficuses, local art and treehouses. With is dense biodiversity this area is home to canopy walks, ziplining and aerial trams. Monteverde has truly taken advantage of all it has to offer.

30- Treehouse Cafe

If you are looking for a truly one of a kind eating

experience, eat in a tree. Sorry I mean a cafe that is wrapped around a tree. The cafe was built around a giant tree, serving as the core of the building with its overhanging branches stretching out of the windows. This dimly lit cafe mimics the cozy atmosphere of picnicking in a tree, something we all wished we could have done as children right?

31- Walk through the Treetops

The Rainmaker Aerial Walkway is the finest example of aerial walkways built in Central America. This canopy tour is still believed to be the best in the region and possibly the country. The highest point on these sturdy walkways brings you 20 stories above the ground. You can walk the area, oscillating low level undergrowth to above the tree canopies, on your own or take a tour guide with you. The tour guide will provide more contextual information to what you are experiencing. There is a wide range of trees and plant life in these parts and Monteverde is known for containing the largest number of orchids in the world, so try not to step on them.

32- Climb the Giant Ficus

Hidden in the surrounded forests of Santa Elena are ficus trees so large they seem like nature's staircase. A long, windy dirt road will bring you from downtown Santa Elena up a hill towards the Monteverde Cloud Forest. It is a secret the locals like keeping from tourists, but ask for directions anyway, everyone who lives there knows where to go and spent their childhood trying to climb their way up to the heavens.

33- Hummingbird Gardens

The drive to the hummingbird gardens is about 20-25 minutes on a rocky road in a chicken bus from Santa Elena. They are called chicken buses because you will often see senoritas bringing on a chicken or two (or sometimes a box of chicks) and will be clucking and squealing with her friends on her ride to the market. Chicken buses are old American school buses the American government gave to Latin America as their form of public transportation—how generous. However, those in Latin America have an incredible tendency to make the best of the little they are given. So instead of the buses remaining the same crayola colored yellow, the locals create their own version of

'Pimp My Ride.' The chicken buses are repainted and decked out to the driver's desire—kaleidoscopic rainbow patterns, murals of the ocean and portraits of their people—turning each one into a wild magic school bus experience. Absolutely take a ride on a chicken bus, though I digress.

You bounce upon an unpaved road and depending on the driver you swerve or sometimes careen on these windy mountain roads, completely lacking all guardrails, traveling farther away from civilization and deeper up the mountainside. Once I stepped off the bus, a metallic snitch whizzed by my head. I turned to see the park entrance, and to its left is a small shop exuding the aromas of pour over coffee and cake (the only two things that get me to do anything really). Then another snitch, this time metallic blue and green, zips by my head, just missing my ear. I walked over to the porch to notice a dozen of these snitches fluttering at magnificent speed from one hanging feeder to the next.

I am reminded of the rare moments I got to see a hummingbird sip the sugar water from the feeder in my grandmother's backyard— right by the sliding glass door in her living room with a view to her outside garden. I would clumsily rush to the window trying to catch a moment of this cartoonish creature. Just seeing one was enough to feed my childlike magic for a week. Now I was surrounded by a dozen of them. However, the ones at home were not nearly as brightly ornamented as the ones congregating around multiple hanging feeders on the porch of the cafe. These were of neon hues of blue, green and purple with metallic shimmers painted across their whole bodies. Colors I didn't know existed in nature. They greedily buzzed from one feeder to the next (and as a sugar addict myself, I can certainly understand) pushing aside other birds to tap whatever was left out of each feeder. At the speed they were moving, it seemed like they would never get enough, always thinking of the next hit, and would bully their way into new feeders. The back and forth between feeders was mesmerizing, and it was a good thing the cafe was closing because I could have stayed there all day, hypnotized by a reality not even my wildest childlike dreams could have created. At the speed they are going, it is amazing to see how they gracefully avoid crashing into things.

34- Coffee Plantations and Tastings

If you are anything like the Finish (or you ARE

Finish) who drink on average 14 cups of coffee daily, I suggest you learn about the process that keeps you together throughout the day. There are two main coffee tours for an afternoon excursion around Monteverde/ Santa Elena: Don Juan Costa Rica or The Café Monteverde Coffee Tour.

Costa Rican coffee is globally renowned due to the ideal climate conditions and soil for coffee plantations. Taking one of the coffee plantation tours will give you a hands on learning experience about the world's favorite beverage. You will learn about the planting process (it takes 3-4 years for a coffee tree to produce fruit) and then walk amongst the fully grown, coffee berry producing trees. The trees are harvested by hand selecting each berry (so THAT is why good coffee is so expensive) because ideal locations for growing coffee is in rugged, mountainous locations, making it difficult to use harvesting machinery. Each plantation needs to be gone through 2-3 times, selectively stripping only the ripe fruits during each round and leaving the ones that still need to ripen further. If you come during October— March, the coffee cherries (yes, that is what they are called) will be bright red and ready to be picked. If you want to come back a coffee snob, try practicing and identifying the different notes and undertones of each coffee. Each one will have bold to soft flavors with undertones of chocolate, fruits, nuts or wine.

35- Aerial Tram

If ziplining isn't your speed, enjoy the aerial sights while calmly skimming the tops of the tree canopy. From such great heights, you will be able to enjoy this diverse ecosystem and experience all of the life that happens atop the forest. This famous cloud forest is home to over 400 species of birds who just might whiz by you on their way to lunch on some of the thousands of insects that also call this forest home.

Good for hiking, birdwatching, canopy tours, ziplining, horseback riding

Chapter 5: San Gerardo de Dota

36- Breathing in a Cloud

For a hidden retreat into the mountains, San Gerardo is a nearby getaway south of the cosmopolitan capital city, San Jose. The village is nestled in an emerald valley, protected and cooled by the Talamanca mountains. The landscape transforms the typical tropical environment from the hot and humid adoring almond trees and magnolias to the cooler climate loving peach trees and strawberry patches.

This cloud forest is remote, so much so that they have no supermarkets, banks, or gas stations. You will be dependent on the lodging to provide food and transportation—making it an ideal spot to get away.

37- Quetzales National Park

The park is named in honor of the quetzale, a tufted aqua blue bird that seems to come out of a Dr. Seuss book. As colorful their plumage is, they are kind of there just for display, being weak flyers, having weak beaks and above all having a bird brain. They also live solitary lives, only hanging out with each other when it is mating season, unlike those social butterflies that also roam the mountainous woodlands. The mating season for the quetzales is from mid-February through July. The park also offers other pseudo-ornithologists numerous opportunities to spot a wide range of other birds. Around 200 mesmerizing bird species are fluttering, flying and speeding through this misty atmosphere, making it hard to get your head out of the clouds... I mean the forest.

Good for- birdwatching, hiking, silence, cloud forests

Caribbean Side—Like mentioned earlier, Costa Rica contains multitudes—like an all you can eat buffet—it caters to every strange craving before you even know what you want. Surfing and rock climbing? Rastafarian beats and salsa? Adventure biking and tropical beaches? Empanadas and a milkshake? Most locations, especially on the coast, provide an opportunity to enjoy the diversity and multiple layers of Costa Rica. However, each area does have its own personality, from the Caribbean, to the Central Valley, and the Pacific coast, each area holds its own Costa Rican flair (enticing you to stay and discover the whole country).

The Caribbean side is the idyllic desktop background that pops up when your coworker has been away from their desk for too long—picking up the day old doughnuts—white sand and turquoise waters with the Talamanca Mountains as the backdrop.

Chapter 6: Tortuguero

Tortuguero is one of those rare corners of the world that are only accessible by plane or boat—a corner mother nature didn't want humans to disrupt, with good reason. Tortuguero, appropriately named 'region of turtles,' is one of the country's dominant and pristine nesting sites for the numerous kinds of sea turtles. It isn't a place you can just drive by... in order to experience the magic of Tortuguero, one surrenders to the remoteness and lack of wifi to truly enjoy an uninterrupted few days in the rich natural beauty of the area. Be one with nature (because there actually isn't that much else to do).

The little village of Tortuguero, which sleeps on a relatively small patch of sand, is coddled between the canals and the Caribbean. On one side lies an interconnected canal and mangrove rainforest and to the front of the village lies the expansive Caribbean ocean.

38- Sea Turtle Mothers, Hatchlings, and Running to Freedom

The beaches around Tortuguero are key nesting sites for four species of sea turtle: hawksbill, loggerheads, green, and leatherbacks. The green are especially sacred because they are on the endangered species list—so even seeing them is a real treasure. They lay their eggs in the winter months and hatch between November and January. If you visit between February and July, you will catch the pregnant turtles surfing in from the far reaching corners of the world to practice the prehistoric ritual of the egg laying on the sands of Tortuguero. Slowly, you will watch them reach land, waddling in off their sea legs and getting their bearings before finding the perfect plot of sand. They relieve themselves of the eggs that their bodies have carried for God knows how many miles across the ocean. This may have been their first time on land after months in the ocean After laying her eggs, sometimes up to 110 eggs in a nest, the mama packs her bags. She does not stay around for the birth of her babies, and gets back to her bigger plans. These are mothers who apparently believe coddling their young makes them soft.

If you decide to visit between November and January, you will be witness to the first ephemeral moments of the lives of these marvelous creatures. The hatchlings usually emerge from their nest at night, making the journey to sea feel somehow sacred and supernatural. After they begin breaking through the protective shells that have been their home for the past few months, the hatchlings take their first few breaths of air. Then without Google maps or any instruction, they are guided by their internal compass to the line that divides the earth and the water. Their purpose is so immediate and unwavering, while we humans wander around the earth philosophizing about our sense of direction in the cosmos, these little guys are like, 'headed for the water—step aside, we're headed straight for the water!'

It is the wobbliest race to the finish line. They ski across the beach, bellies leaving chaotic lines in the sand, formed by survival, youth and grit. The stakes are high. For those who do hatch, only 1% will survive until adulthood. Immediately faced with obstacles and natural enemies, many don't make it, thwarted by seagulls and other predators between their nests and the ocean. As you cheer them on and witness this bewitching sight of the winners floating out to sea, you can't help but feel a sense of excitement for new life, the adventures that await them in the big blue sea, and the hopeful return to their homeland to continue the cycle.

39- Learn More about Turtles

If you are interested in learning more about the turtles and the surrounding area, there is the Caribbean Conservation Corporation Visitor Center and Museum in Tortuguero village, a sweet little local information center. It offers a wide range of knowledge about all of the creatures that inhabit the area. All funds go toward turtle conservation and protection.

40- Glide Through Central America's Amazon

The second largest attraction to in the area is Tortuguero Plain. Behind Tortuguero, lies an expansive biodiverse macrocosm, nicknamed 'Central America's Amazon.'

The waterways interlink and pass through lagoons and lakes giving you hours of peaceful paddling in your canoe. The coastal wetlands and mangroves shape the canals as these trees twist and twine their roots together, creating the tropical rainforest. The plant life is extremely diverse.

Try passing through these serene waterways like a scavenger hunt. There is a plethora of biodiverse wildlife and endangered species that I want you to try to identify that will be camouflaged in the wild mangrove. See how many you can find!

There are local tours that will take you out boating for a few hours through the tranquil canals with a guide identifying and teaching you about the natural phenomenon. These tours take place on a motor boat and will give a general overview of the area. Count how many species you can find—some are truly rare and special sightings, so keep your eyes peeled.

Who makes up the mangrove? Floating aquatic plants, gavilán, the endangered caobilla almendro and the endangered monkey pot tree.

Who is in the canal? Manatees, caimans, crocodiles, and tropical gar. Fish include: cichlidae, characidae, pimelodidae, carcharinidae, centropomidae, and lutjanidae.

Who is climbing in the mangrove? Jaguars, three-toed sloths, and monkeys, including the Geoffroy's spider, the mantled howler, and the white-headed capuchin. Basilisk lizards and poisonous frogs, iguanas

Who is in the sky? Kingfishers, toucans, blue herons, peacocks, and parrots, crested eagles, and salamanders.

41- Paddle Your Own Canoe

If you are craving freedom from tourists and tour guides, you can rent a boat and paddle your own canoe or kayak! Going out on your own boat is a quieter way to explore, and allows you explore some of the harder-to-reach areas and setting your own schedule. Go make your own adventure through the mangrove!

42- Night Tours

If you are interested in experiencing the darker

side of the jungle, I suggest doing a night boat tour through the canals. It offers an inverse experience of the creatures and plants that make up the jungle, sort of like the jungle in the upside down (Stranger Things). You'll meander down the waterways in darkness while the tour guide shines a spotlight to illuminate crocodiles, frogs, caimans, crabs and bats. See if you can catch a glimpse of the nocturnal animals that inhabit the waterways before they disappear back into the depths of the jungle.

43- Hiking Tortuguero Hill

If you are looking to stretch your legs after sitting in a boat for several hours, take a hike on Tortuguero Hill. Tortuguero Hill is the highest point on the Caribbean side of Costa Rica The two hour hike offers breathtaking aerial views of the area. An alternative hike is the two-mile Gavilan Trail. This trail offers more intimate, quiet moments with the jungle surroundings. Remember you will be walking through wetlands, so it would be wise to grab a pair of rubber boots before entering.

44- Be Amongst the Treetops

Canopy tour and ziplining—Just because everyone comes here for the turtles, it doesn't mean there is nothing else to do. Why not take the aerial view and observe the beaches crowded with people snapchatting their favorite hatchlings from a distance. There are several tours that will have you feel like you are walking through the canopy on very stable elevated bridges that connect you to the animals at the top of the forest. If you're looking for more of an adrenaline rush, then absolutely do some ziplining.

45- Sport Fishing

Sport fishing has become increasingly popular. Go out on a tour boat farther into the ocean and try your best bet at small game fishing. Some lodges will even let you cook what you catch. Study up and know in advance what types of fish you are interested in, as they tend to congregate in slightly different areas. Grab a bag of night crawlers and see if you can catch some of the following fish (depending on the season).

- Tarpon (Sabalo)—season is from January to June

- Bass—from September to December.

- Macarela and Barracuda—tend to be closer to the coast.

- Marlin, Sailfish and Tuna—in copious quantities offshore.

- Crushed Bass and Rainbow Bass—if you do river fishing.

There is no limit to how much you can relax on the beach here. Do be careful as the waves and surf here tend to be stronger than in other areas of Costa Rica.

46- Birdwatching

If you are interested in more than what is found in the sea, and are intrigued by the life in the sky, go on a bird walking tour. Whip out your pretentious binoculars and handcrafted notebook like the wannabe ornithologist you are and get to work identifying over 300 bird species native to the area, like green ibis, great potoo, scarlet macaw, green macaw, and kingfishers. These are just a sampling of the species that you can encounter on an organized tour or on your own excursions.

Good for beaches, hiking, canoeing/kayaking, canopies, ziplining, fishing, animal interactions, diverse plants.

Chapter 7: Limon

47- Lounging in Limon

A city on the edge of the Caribbean that used to be more of an important epicenter. It is currently still the country's most important port—providing the quickest trade routes to other areas around the globe. The tribal Bribri people populated the region for thousands of years before the conquistadors literally blew into it. In 1502, a hurricane forced Christopher Columbus to anchor his weathered ships on Uvita Island off the coast of Costa Rica during his exploration of the New World. He and his crew ventured onto the mainland and founded what is now modern Puerto Limón. For this, Puerto Limon holds the title as one of the oldest cities on the continent (by Western perception) and takes pride in the historical significance and imperative ports in the city.

This isn't someplace to spend a weekend, but is a good overnight stop if you are going from Tortuguero to Puerto Viejo and are looking for a place that has more of a city feel but still allows access to the beach.

Although it provides excellent access to the Atlantic and trade routes, the city has also been affected by numerous earthquakes and some areas are a bit rundown. However, Puerto Limon makes up for it with some intricate architecture and prismatic open air marketplaces lined with colorful fruits and handmade blankets. The main market in the center of town is the place to go to buy everything from wood carved items to traditional souvenirs. The city is surrounded by cashew trees, so be sure to sample or grab a bottle of their specialty cashew wine. Take a walk through the jungle-ish park of Balvanera Vargas where people and sloths alike hangout and watch the day drip by.

48- Oxtail

If you are getting a little hungry or itching for a nibbling of merendar (afternoon snack), there are numerous restaurants and cafes that offer meals with a cultural combination of Tico cuisine infused with

Caribbean spices. Stop by Caribbean Kalisi Coffee Shop—the staff speaks English in their spacious, clean restaurant with authentic Caribbean food. Definitely try the oxtail with tres leches cake or arroz con leche with a big cup of local coffee for dessert.

49- Get Down with Rastafarian Beats, Spanish Pop or Swinging Salsa

While the city is rather laid back during the day, at night Puerto Limon has quite an active social scene. There are a number of bars and restaurants found all over the city, giving it a reputation for an active and diverse nightlife. From salsa dancing, to Rastafarian clubbing or Spanish pop songs, there is a club here for every style and swing.

50- Playa Bonita

If the sounds of the city begin to wear you down and you want to heal your sore body from a night of dancing—hail down a bus to Playa Bonita. This is a popular surfing beach for Puerto Limon residents and is a quick drive from the city limits. Playa Bonita offers good surfing or meditation opportunities (aka naps) to the sound of the waves.

51- Dia de Las Culturas

The city holds several large cultural festivals throughout the year, so if the stars align with your schedule try to join in on the festivities. The best time to visit Puerto Limon is around Columbus Day, for Dia de las Culturas. It is an annual jubilation celebration of the discovery of the New World by Christopher Columbus. This annual carnival is the biggest event in Limon and is celebrated with huge parades, loud music and parties that tumble onto the streets. You will be finding confetti on your body for weeks.

52- Festival of Flowers

If you time your visit right, during the summer is the Festival of Flowers of the African Diaspora. This festival is as colorful as it sounds. It is supported by the Foundation for Culture and Art Development, a non-profit organization based in Costa Rica, whose work is dedicated to the protecting the cultural rights of all Central American ethnic diversities and celebrating the beautiful multiculturalism of these cultures. The festival is a well-rounded description of the cultural blending and influence of the region with art, culture and fashion exhibitions and obviously tons of great food. The Festival of Flowers is aimed to provide general knowledge to the public of the cultural richness of all peoples.

Good for Caribbean culture, Caribbean food, beaches, shopping, music, nightlife, coffee, chocolate, festivals, and pura vida.

Playa Cahuita—If you are making your way from Limon to Puerto Viejo, and are looking to replace the noise of nightlife with wildlife, take an afternoon to stop at Playa Cahuita. Playa Cahuita is a quiet, Rastafarian influenced town with stunning white sand. Cahuita National Park is more of a water park than anything else. The snorkeling and diving offer a wide range of underwater adventures with opportunities to interact with a wide variety of marine life, giving you a chance to slow down and savor the sights of the second best coral reef in the world.

53- Eating Authentically at Miss Edith's

If you find yourself hungry, definitely check out restaurants in this area. The area has Caribbean island influence (are you noticing a pattern here), so the food here is not the typical Tico dish. If you are looking for a truly authentic cuisine (including authentic slow-paced service) get breakfast or lunch at Miss Edith's. Here you will have more than traditional rice and beans, everything contains the added flair of Latin spices—rice cooked in coconut milk, garlic seafood and homemade ginger brews.

54- Dance with Chiquita Bananas

Banana plantations are nearby—one of Costa Rica's largest exports. Go walking through acres of bananas and witness how the fruit is grown and harvested. Del Monte and Chiquita both allow tours of their banana plantations. Bananito farm is located about 20 minutes south of Limon. The plantations pride themselves on demonstrating leadership in producing environmentally and socially sound productions systems and agricultural practices. As you walk through (and snag a banana or two as you are walking around) you will see the whole banana production system—propping, bagging, harvesting, and packing, In addition, the agency may request specially tailored presentations for groups whose members have particular interests.

Good for snorkeling, diving, beaches, and a strong Caribbean influence.

55- Reserva Biológica Hitoy Cerere

Hitoy-Cerere is a bit off the beaten track. This center is under the radar for a lot of tourists, making it an ideal way to get away from all the gringos, allowing you to submerge in the untouched wilderness teeming with regional animals, and is ideal for birdwatching. The plethora of natural waterways are formed due to intense rainfall, in conjunction with uneven terrain, making this park a fun adventure to enjoy on horseback, and thus making them do all the work. Additionally, the park is home to numerous isolated indigenous reserves, giving you a peek into Costa Rican life before the rise of Westernization and ecotourism.

Good for indigenous culture, horseback riding, birdwatching, and hiking.

Chapter 8: Puerto Viejo

56- Caribbean Pura Vida

On the opposite end of the Caribbean coast, on the border of Panama, lies Puerto Viejo. On the other side of the Caribbean coin, Puerto Viejo's bouncing energy contrasts the tranquility of Tortuguero. Where Tortuguero cultivates quiet introspection and intimacy with nature, Puerto Viejo cultivates intimate moments with the locals, the country's favorite rum, Ron Centenario, and sometimes the toilet. Puerto Viejo is a simmering stew of cultures and energies, a blending of Spanish, West Indies, expats, Jamaica and native influences.

The town is like a giant living room—people are barefoot, lounging around smoking cigarettes and drinking coffee all day, and meanwhile smells of jerk chicken and coconut rice waft through the air so intensely it feels like you are standing in the kitchen of the Tico mother you never had. The town, cradled by the water's edge, shaded by palm and coconut trees, with colorful sarongs and towels ornamenting the trees and buildings like a tropical Christmas. The open air architecture of the town allows anyone to be inside and outside simultaneously and shout out their windows to neighbors in order to continue the town's continual conversation. The buildings are half exposed to the outdoors, but although the weather is fantastic for most of the year, the locals live each day like it is the first day of summer, truly appreciative of the continuous presence of the sun.

What really makes this area unique is the intermingling of the variety of cultures. The native Bribri and Cabecar costumes, Jamaican and West Indian Rastafarian rhythms and philosophies, plus the Spanish language turn Puerto Viejo into an congenial microcosm—where all types of people live harmoniously by the sea. The number one adventure is to have a real conversation with a stranger. Pick their brain about what it is like to live there and learn their perception of the world.

57- Arise with the Madrugar

Okay, I am always one for sleeping in, especially on vacations, but don't deny yourself the experience of a spectacular madrugar—to rise early to see the sunrise. These sunsets and sun rises are some of the best in the world—like a giant sherbert sunday melting into the ocean. It's easy to get lost in what the Japanese call boketto—to gaze vacantly into the distance without thinking. Then turn right around and go get yourself some of the best, locally-sourced coffee in the world.

Town—So you have just begun exploring Puerto Viejo and are a little overwhelmed with how much there is to experience and don't know where to start. How can such a tiny town be packed with so many things to do?! I don't have enough time! If I had a superpower it would be to capture time and release it whenever I needed it. I never feel like I have enough time. Let's relax, maintain our focus, grab a quick cup of coffee before you start your adventures, and periodically take a moment to just be. Fortunately, you are in one of the top coffee producing cultures in the world, so you know it will be good. Personally, I rank my favorite locations by coffee shops, and Puerto Viejo is pretty high on the list. The locals take advantage of the top quality coffee produced in the central valley and brew a damn fine pour over for your taste of Puerto Viejo's pura vida delights.

58- Coffee, Java & Chocolate

Caribeans, Chocolate and Coffee—If before this trip, you have been day-dreaming into the eyes of monkeys on the packaging of the $12 chocolate bars at Whole Foods, you can finally meet it at the source. I suggest heading straight to Caribeans Chocolate and Coffee. This place is a baker's delight. They make their own organic fair trade chocolate here that you can stick in your pocket and slowly indulge on throughout the day. They offer a wide variety of dessert coffee drinks, cakes, and latte art for that oh-so-perfect Instagram picture you've been craving to take since the moment you landed, (remember, calories don't count when you are on vacation).

Bread & Chocolate—Does the title need to say more? This place provides generous portions of locally sourced fruits, baked goods, towering sandwiches and damn good coffee, right on the water's edge. This is another great spot to indulge your sweet tooth. They have wonderful fresh baked muffins, breads, and chocolate cakes.

Cafe Rico—Upon walking into Cafe Rico, you might think you accidentally stumbled into someone's personal library (which in Puerto Viejo is totally possible, it is often hard to tell the difference between a restaurant and someone's kitchen in these parts). This philosopher's delight is lined with hundreds of books for your reading pleasure as you enjoy a bountiful breakfast of fresh fruit, eggs, garlic potatoes, and pancakes. Grab a book that peaks your interest while you watch your food be prepared in an open air kitchen. Now that you are copacetic after your first taste of Puerto Viejo, it is time to explore.

59- Biking

Personally, I believe there is no better way to enjoy a new location than by bike. It is the Goldilocks form of transportation—not as slow as walking when there is a lot of area to cover, but not as fast as driving where it is a pain to stop and park at every little thing that intrigues you. Biking gives you the freedom to go at your own pace and stop whenever you want to linger a moment longer or follow a curiosity. You are traveling at the ideal perspective for exploration and are free to observe the area at a level that human height sometimes denies you.

I rented a bike in Puerto Viejo and it was the best money I spent. I was able to reach areas that I couldn't have just by walking. Once I was on the bike, I felt such immediate freedom and just started peddling. Like fingers gently touching a Ouija board, I felt the bike assume its own direction without my influence. It was listening to my inner compass and tapped into my desire to find the secrets of the area. My joyride took me to areas I couldn't have accessed by foot or car, sometimes ending up in beautiful backyards, personal gardens, or hidden ocean coves.

At one point, my joy ride leads me to a semi-exposed overgrown field with white and gray horses peacefully grazing in the middle, the jungle providing a lush a backdrop to their munching. I paused to meditate in the moment, the swishing and swaying of their tails, together, composed a syncopated music like brushes on drums, adding the backbeat to the rhythms of the jungle. Suddenly, out of the peace came chaos. A deep guttural roar howled through the air, like the brief warning characters in movies receive when the monster is nearby. My body tensed and I dropped my bike. WTF IS THAT? Then silence. Then a scream came out again, a response to the call. The serenity of the moment had been usurped and my fight or flight mode was activated (DANGER. DANGER, WILL ROBINSON.) However, I found myself more curious than scared and felt myself turn into all the dumb characters in horror movies whose curiosity gets the best of them while you are screaming at the television, "DON'T GO THERE!" I stepped off the pavement and into the field, wondering if maybe the horses were the ones making such a cacophony, though I couldn't pinpoint the beings that were making the noise. Then I spotted another biker, lazily peddling towards me. I rush up to them in the middle of the road and scream, "A MONSTER IS COMING," (in embarrassingly broken Spanish), "UNO MONSTRO VENIR." The rider paused, straddling her bike and listened. Then after hearing the horrible sound, without response, her shoulders started laughing, "Oh you gringa, that is just a howler monkey, they aren't going to hurt you! Tranquillo!" She went on her way, and continued to push one pedal at a time. I went back to my own spot, with a clear view of the horses, still undisturbed by the sounds of monsters that roamed above them, and wished I could have that sense of stillness in the midst of such chaos.

I continued my biking journey, and was able to stop and explore any lightly treaded paths to the ocean, taking moments to stare out into the sea, before heading back to the village.

60- Surf the Salsa Brava

Puerto Viejo is one of the top destinations for surfing, and hosts some of the most popular surf competitions in the world. In the past, people have flocked to surf at the 2014 Olympus National Surfing Circuit—Lime Coral Caribbean Classic II and the 2016 Kolbi National Surfing Circuit.

Salsa Brava is considered to be the biggest break in all of Costa Rica. This Caribbean style wave works the best during the dry season (November through April). Salsa Brava translates to 'angry sauce' and you can only imagine why. It is a style of wave that gains momentum out in the deep water and breaks over the shallow reef situated at the feet of the village. Don't get too ambitious or arrogant—you don't want to spend your vacation in a hospital.

If you still want to get some great surfing in, but feel like keeping your body in one piece, Playa Cocles is your safer option. Right around the corner from Salsa Brava, Cocles receives a strong swell from the northeast, ranging from a head to overhead height. At this end, the waves are more manageable and as you lay on the sand you can Instagram picturesque views of the giant rocks not so far from sea that are covered with trees. You will have a great workout as you ebb back and forth with the waves, playing peekaboo with the rocks sprinkled in the distance, bobbing in the middle of the ocean, but remember the locals have been working these waves since they could crawl onto a surfboard. If you are a lover of surfing or have always been curious, the swell in Puerto is an authentic experience.

61- Hangout with the Cast of the Little Mermaid

Take a boat out to explore the reef that embroiders the edges of Puerto Viejo. There are plenty of tour companies where you can rent a mask or that will take you out diving. While you are submerged, count how many of these underwater beauties you see!

Lionfish, starfish sea rods, sea fans, elk horn coral, brain coral, fire coral, and tropical fish, like the parrot fish, angel fish, scorpion fish, barracuda, butterfly fish, trunkfish, spotted eagle ray, green moray, evasive nurse shark and blacktip Shark. If you decide to go out at night, you have a chance to see the ocean on the hunt, watch sharks, crabs and octopus come out and feast upon a seafood banquet.

If you don't want to take a tour and explore on your own, sneak off to Punta Uva, the heart of the Gandoca Manzanillo National Wildlife Refuge. You can leave behind those creatures who walk on two feet and pretend you are a mermaid swimming with the colorful rainbow of fish, coral and aquatic creatures.

62- Petting Jungle Kitties

Want to find a way to get your agoraphobic cat-obsessed best friend to Costa Rica? Bring her to The Jaguar Rescue Center! It was opened in 2008 by primatologist couple. Jaguars are not the only animals that call this center their home; as you wander through you will spot other typical Costa Rican wildlife living out their daily routines. Monkeys bobbing in and out of the trees, snakes camouflaged on the ground, frogs playing hop scotch, sloths slowly reaching for a quick-moving insect, and a full chorus of birds singing at every octave. The rescue center provides details about how animals are reintroduced to the wild, whenever possible.

If you are on a quest for something dangerous but rewarding, take the night tour and witness the liveliness of the jungle while everyone else is fast asleep. You can really get your blood pumping when you watch the midnight buffet as some of the most powerful predators come out to feast. I can't guarantee you will see any feasting, and I'm not sure of the chances of you watching a jaguar stalk, pounce and devour its prey, as exciting as that would be. The most feasting you may actually see is a sloth munching on a leaf for fifteen minutes.

63- Chocolate Forests

If you can down a chocolate sheet cake in a minute and really came to Costa Rica because you want to believe that there is a chocolate waterfall somewhere in the world for you to plunge yourself into, then you have to take a tour at CariBeans. This fine chocolate establishment walks you through their chocolate forest. They show you the rusty colored cacao pods through different stages of growth, how they are harvested, processed, fermented and transformed into the food of the gods.

However, this is more than the Willy Wonka's Chocolate Factory of your childhood dreams. The staff takes pride in making organic, fair trade chocolate and they work alongside local indigenous population to ensure that the restoration of the cacao farm is ecologically balanced and sustainable. So, no guilt as you polish off your 3rd chocolate bar of the day, you are saving the planet.

64- Drinks and Dancing

After long lazy days on the beach and endless coconut rice and beans, the Puerto Viejo locals flat get happening at night. There is no need to 'research' where to go, just listen to which building has the loudest music. The nightlife feels like a house party, each street is a different room and people are bouncing in and out of the few, but wild, options in the town. If you choose to stay in one room, there are several different types of nighttime entertainment. There plenty of opportunities to get on the dance floor, drink a few Tumba Calzones to get up the courage to ask the cute local to take salsa lessons with you at the dance clubs, with breathtaking views of the stars lighting up the beach. Or if you prefer, there are relaxed Reggae cocktail bars with a rainbow of lounge chairs for you and your friends to occupy while you are comfortably sipping Jaguar Coladas until you are into a complete stupor. The guaro cocktail comes with maracuyá (passionfruit) and coconut crème. There are also live bands and DJ sets where you can jump and slosh your Malacrianza Beer all over the dance floor. They go all night, ebullient with the energy they received from all those rice and beans.

Good for nightlife, shopping, chocolate tours, animal reserves, hiking, biking, horseback riding, and surfing.

Conclusion to Caribbean Coast

Your journey from the north to south end of the Caribbean coast will hopefully be filled with more adventures than are provided here. I hope you have gotten a taste of the spicy influence of the island and maybe have been seduced enough to stay like some expats who say things like, "I came here for a weekend and stayed for 12 years." Hopefully, when you do return home you will take with you the spirit of pura vida; but ideally, you won't have returned at all.

Chapter 9: Pacifico Norte

The Pacific side offers just as much as the Caribbean side, but with a different prerogative. This coast is closer to both main airports in Liberia and San Jose and is more developed than its Rastafarian brother. The Pacific side has more overdeveloped beach towns, lining the beaches with more bars, hotels, and night clubs than the typical small isolated towns with one grocery store and bar on the Caribbean side. The roads are also marked better and paved, making transportation faster, and catering to the spillover of tourists booking from the airport.

The natural wealth is different here—everything is bigger. The schools of iridescent fish on the Caribbean side turn into dolphins, sharks and humpback whales on the Pacific side. The diving gets deeper, the parks more expansive, the hills become volcanos , and the cabanas become resorts.

The Pacific coast allows you to waste no time between its beaches and forests; this side has half a dozen national parks braided in between its shores. Those looking for resorts, college-educated tour guides and upscale dining will be more copacetic with their options here, but the sometimes elaborate beach towns and tourist prices might not be best suited for those who are looking for a quieter experience with nature.

Let the Adventure Begin in Liberia—If you start your adventure on the Pacific side, you will most likely be arriving in the north western city of Liberia, either by driving from Nicaragua or by flying into the airport. Although this relaxed city tends to be more of a launching pad to the pacific coast there are still simple delights in this city as you pick magnolias along the sidewalks or a mango on the street from a tree that is falling over the fence. Here, nature cannot be contained.

65- El Museo de Sabanero

Liberia is home to sabanero culture, home of the Costa Rican cowboy. Ranching took off once the conquistadors introduced horses to the new world and was ideal in the now Guanacaste province due to the sunny dry climate, rolling plains that roll up to the statuesque volcanos, and mountains that make up the Guanacaste Range.

Visit "El Museo de Sabanero" located in a traditional colonial-era house, Casa de Culture. The house is ornamented with a sizeable collection of lassos and saddle-ware (including many decorated saddles), spurs, lanterns, and also includes pictures and history from throughout the years. Resist the urge to bring your plastic Disney Toy Story toys, this is the real thing.

66- Cowboy for a Day

A great day trip from Liberia is Hacienda Guachipelin, 15.5 miles from Liberia, offering seven different horseback riding tours on the trails to the Rincon de la Vieja National Park, giving you a chance to get up close and personal with 'Costa Rica's best all-terrain vehicle—the horse.' The bucolic trails lead you to and through the dry tropical rainforest of the park stopping at waterfalls or natural thermal springs.

If you would like a chance to walk in the boots of the sabaneros for a day, and have always wanted a taste of the cowboy life since you watched Woody ride like the wind with Bullseye, you can live out your rodeo dreams at Hacienda Guachipelin. The ecotourist hacienda offers a 'Cowboy for a Day' tour, where you meet and assist real sabaneros around the farm. Milk cows, tend to the stables and corral, saddle and ready the horses, and ride out into the fields to herd cattle or horses. Just don't go rogue and gallop off into the sunset never to return. Instead, leave the cliché's for the travel writers.

Good for horseback riding, ranching, hikes, lick and a promise.

Parks of Guanacaste and Peninsula de Nicoya

67- Nature's Spa Day at Rincon de la Vieja Volcan

Rincon de la Vieja and Santa Rosa National parks— both part of UNESCO Area de Conservación

Guanacaste—are vast lands that are home to an intermingling of different biomes. The parks of this area are like walking through several of the biomes described in your 6th grade earth science book, ranging from mangrove woodlands, savannas, deciduous forest, cloud forests and the ocean. It is incredible to believe all of these temperatures can coexist so closely in one area. These areas are best explored either by foot or horseback.

Rincon de La Vieja has enough personality to overwhelm one for a day; the area bleeds together numerous biospheres, offering exposure to volcanos, waterfalls, geothermal phenomenon, cloud forests, dry tropical forests and mineral lakes.

The apexes of the Rincon de la Vieja and Santa Maria volcanoes, are the focal points of this dry tropical park. These two andesitic sister volcanoes reign supreme in the relatively flat area they occupy, looking down upon the mortals that climb them.

The Guatuso, an ancient indigenous tribe, has a legend that gives the Rincon de la Vieja volcano her name—the old woman's corner. Rincon believes that an old woman makes her home at the volcano's apex. She became a recluse when her father threw her lover into the mouth of the volcano. She receded from civilization and, chose that to be her new home, mourning her lost love for all of eternity. When she is happy—the smoldering heat from the volcano is evidence of her cooking meals for weary travelers. When the volcano is erupting—she is angry and releasing her wrath onto the surrounding environment and people.

This area is bubbling with geothermic activity—from steam vents, geysers and boiling mud pots—Mother Nature's day spa. When you are done be sure to get your nails touched up by a puma—they always have the best gossip and are quick at their job.

Enter through Las Pailas—the cauldrons; or Las Hornillas—the burner; for the royal treatment. There are several trails that take you through the park. Be careful not to get too close unless you are looking for a natural mud facial or steam bath. Some of these trails include mineral baths in pristine pools of water, formed by cascading waterfalls, where you can close your pores from the geysers and fumaroles.

Animals to see include: sloths, tapirs, kinkajous, pumas, jaguar, howler monkeys, and spider monkeys.

Good for forest canopy tours, horseback riding, river rafting, all-terrain-vehicle riding and wall-climbing.

68- Walking on the Battlefields of Santa Rosa National Park

Close to Rincon de la Vieja is the Santa Rosa National Park. This park has won many badges being the first national park of Costa Rica. It is a historical battle site and boasts an assortment of different natural habitats: savannas, deciduous forest, marshlands, tropical and subtropical dry broadleaf forests, mangrove woodlands and the Pacific Ocean. You can go for the history and learn about the Battle of Santa Rosa against the army from Nicaragua and walk on the old battle grounds. Of course this occurred while the country still maintained an army.

Look for coyotes, peccaries, white-nosed coatis, Baird's tapirs, sea turtles, and terrestrial turtles. The three species of monkey are Geoffroy's spider monkey, mantled howler and white-headed capuchin.

A real treasure would be to spot the big cats of the park, including: jaguarundi, ocelot, cougar and jaguar.

69- Paddle Along in Palo Verde National Park

Volcanos are magnificent but they aren't for everyone. The wetland sanctuary of Palo Verde National Park is a shorter drive from Liberia if you are still interested in visiting a multi-ecosystem with more rivers and fewer opportunities to fall into a lava pit visit. A land ruled more by water than fire, Palo Verde's sloping limestone hills recline into a medley of different habitats, including: mangrove swamps, grassy savannahs, marshes, pastures and evergreen forests with the Tempisque River running through the heart of it. The wide range of ecosystems caters to an even wider range of bird species, making it one of the best bird sanctuaries in the country. Take a boat tour or paddle on your own through the Tempisque River and calmly fill your memory bank (or iPhone) with images of over 300 different types of birds or other wildlife.

Good for bird sightings, kayaking or canoeing, and hiking.

Animals include: herons, storks, howler monkeys, American crocodiles, spoonbills, and coatimundis.

70- Cave Diving in Barra Honda National Park

Barra Honda National Park nurtures some of the world's last standing dry tropical forests. However, the natural wealth of the tropical forest conceals the real magic underneath it. This park contains Costa Rica's only subterranean park—a labyrinth of limestone caverns. It has taken 70 million years to form these caves, showing that Mother Nature is in no rush to create a pièce de résistance. The features of the deep limestone caverns are like an upside down mirror of the land directly above it—giant plunging stalactites and stalagmites hanging below the sky, reaching trees and cacti, and exchanging land roaming monkeys for cave dwelling bats.

Much is still unknown about these hollowed out holes in the earth —only a handful have been fully explored, the remainders still harbor more questions and secrets. Barra Honda is a genuine caving experience—one of the few gems that is still under the radar and doesn't cater towards wide-scale tourism. The area is a must if you're driving from San José to Guanacaste. See what it is like to experience the underworld—the life beneath our feet that we all tend to forget even exists.

Good for cave dives and bats; entrance to the underworld.

Beaches of Guanacaste and Peninsula de Playa Nicoya—If you arrive in Liberia, want to skip the forest and start working on your tan right away, there are plenty of beaches close enough to drive to. The beaches offer just as much magic and mystery as the parks that surround them.

71- Sea Caves of Playa Ventanas

The quiet crescent shaped beach of Playa Ventana holds secret sea caves. The beach contains towering rock formations that have gaping holes through them-like being able to travel through the hole in a bead. At low tide, you are able to venture through them—like stepping into a black hole. Theses naturally eroded tunnels shut you out of the tropical surroundings, transporting you to a barren planet, with nothing but the bright light at the end of the tunnel to guide you. Once you enter the mouth of the cave, only the balmy wind accompanies you as once loud waves, throwing themselves upon the rock, turns into a muffled crash. On the other side, your memory will be whipped and you will suddenly have aged by 10 years.

Good for beaches, jungle, and time travel.

72- Dead Men Tell No Tails on Bahia de los Piratas

Bahia de los Piratas is a clandestine piece of coast with rose-tinted sand that used to be used as a hiding spot for Pirates. This beach still leaves one with the feeling of being shipwrecked, with just one solitary hotel. (And wtf is Johnny Depp doing here?) In the distance, a skull and crossbones flag is visible out on a lonely island, broken off from shore, and beckoning you to venture out, reminding you of the lawless creatures it once mislead. Who knows what buried treasure lies under these waters? I would advise you to bring a metal detector, but don't be disappointed if the only booty found is some Australian money, a lost belly button ring or a muffin tin. Be advised to bring your own snacks—and don't freak out when all of the rum is gone.

Good for kayaking, paddle boarding, doubloons, snorkeling, and horseback riding.

Chapter 10: Diving in Guanacaste

73- Octopus Hunting off the Catalina Islands

Beyond Flamingo Bay, Guanacaste, floating off the Pacific coast are the Catalina Islands. These rogue pieces of vegetative land have a magnetic pull for a wide variety of marine life—attracting sea turtles, octopus, eagle rays, moray eels, seahorses, white tip reef sharks, and more. Exploring these areas is a snorkeler or diver's delight as you spend a day or afternoon jumping back and forth between the islands and aquatic explorations.

Good for snorkeling, diving, boat rides, and islands.

74- The Rainbow Fish off the Gulf

This quaint little gulf is the quintessential location for people just hoping to relax, with the typical adventures Costa Rica has to offer. Coconut and palm trees line the wide beaches, providing shade to sunbathers and expansive panoramic views from the beach—from sunrise to sunset. The calm waters and plethora of coral make it a snorkeling destination. Papagayo is a perfect place to enjoy nature and relax. The surrounding government maintains this area's natural integrity, keeping the land pristine and making it great to hike through the lush tropical landscape and over 400 species of wildlife. It is a great location to visit if you don't want to do a lot of traveling and prefer to stay in one spot.

Good for snorkeling, swimming, hiking, and birdwatching

Tranquilo en Tamarindo—Tamarindo, aka 'Tamagringo,' is a vivacious one stop shop for all coastal dreams. The town sleeps on Playa Tamarindo, a mile-long crescent beach, which feels like having a giant swimming pool for your front lawn. The shallow waters make it ideal to sunbathe, play water games and learn to surf. There are restaurants and lounge bars that have front row seating to the ocean if saltwater gives you a bad hair day. After a long day of surfing, shopping in the organic natural shops and tanning on the beach, cozy up on the sand with a blanket with a guaro sour and watch the inflamed sun cool itself into the horizon.

75- Noshing at the Farmers Market

On Saturday mornings, pick up breakfast at the farmer's market, which offers samplings of local fruits, vegetables and souvenir items. I dare you to try as many local foods as possible; the quality and freshness will be superb. Here are a few ideas to experiment and munch on—yuca, chayotes, rambutan and my favorite, the mangosteen. Crack open a mangosteen which resemble the 'more lives' charms in video games.

Lastly, you better ingest some tamarind while you are staying here, either raw, cooked or in a soda. How can you miss the experience of eating the fruit which the town takes its name from. No tamarind in

Tamarindo, would be like not eating turkey in Turkey— wait, the Middle East doesn't have— nevermind.

Playa Tamarindo calls out to all the surfer dudes, challenging them to take on Pico Pequeño, a rock-ribbed point that sometimes has waves reaching 12 feet, challenging even the most aggressive of surfers.

76- Turtle Tours at Playa Grande

Tamarindo is juxtaposed the white sand beaches of Playa Grande. These beaches are sacred spaces to both the locals and the leatherback turtles that come to lay their eggs. From November to April, you can burn a whole night waiting patiently for the mother turtles to surf to ashore to lay their eggs. Then from June-September cheer on your favorite little hatchling and hope it makes it out to sea. Tamarindo and Playa Grande are separated by the Tamarindo River (Playa Grande turned to Tamarindo, "I feel like there is something between us…") but you can jump on a ferry which will take you to the other side.

Good for ATV tours, horseback riding, kayaking, white water rafting or tubing, volcano tours, scuba diving, snorkeling, sport fishing, sailing, surfing, turtle tours, ziplining, canopy tours, shopping.

77- Surfing the Big Surf

Guiones has basically become a synonym for surfing and is one of the top destinations in Costa Rica for it. The white sand beach that expands for four miles catches most swells year-round. The waters are ideal for learning how to surf—rhythmic, rolling waves that tend to drop down gently, ranging from knee-high to double-overhead. The steady topography maintains the swell and keeps the waves from becoming too aggressive, which is ideal for newcomers or those who are looking for a good surf—not a challenge. The result is some of the most reliable surf in the world. The surf community is a nurturing environment for beginners, as well.

At low tide, the entire Guiones bay area can be explored by bicycle or on foot. The beach is also part of a conservation zone, Reserva Biológica Nosara, allowing great access to the jungles behind the bay. If you would like to stretch out after hitting the waves, there are numerous yoga studios where you can take your mat right out on the beach or venture to rooftops and watch the sunset as you are doing your own sun salutations.

Good for surfing, yoga, hikes, biking, and chillin.'

Chapter 11: Península de Nicoya

Now we are going to venture down the peninsula to slightly more secluded areas of Costa Rica. Peninsula de Nicoya is a rich piece of land sprinkled with colorful coastal towns like a slice of birthday cake. Say goodbye to your touristy friends from Tamarindo who believe that Costa Rica is 'just one big beach' and step out into rugged roads and rocky beaches of the undomesticated tropical land.

78- Surfing and Seclusion of Mal País & Santa Teresa

After the tourist traps of Tamarindo, make your way down the Nicoya Peninsula to the more authentic sleepy towns on the leg of Costa Rica. Since you are taking the time to adventure into these more remote areas—be sure to hit the coastal couplet of Santa Teresa and Mal Pais.

This secluded slice of paradise is a bit off the beaten path and where the Tico's go to surf—so you know it is good. Here, you won't be bumping into pasty amateur teenagers on spring break, rail-banging themselves and messing with your flow. The quiet seclusion and quality swell of Santa Teresa and Mal Pais are ideal places for you to practice your back slides or aerials. However, as of recently, there has been an uptick in gringos visiting these quiet bohemian boroughs.

Good for beaches, surfing, jungle, hiking, animals, and chillin.'

79- Cabo Blanco National Park

For some quiet introspection, the surrounding forests of Cabo Blanco National Park serve as an ideal location. Cabo Blanco is one of the first protected parks in the country, due to the heavy 'development,' (cut to the Lorax drowning in his own tears), in the early 1960's. Since then, the government has don't a full 180 degree turn and implemented legislation protecting these sacred forests. As part of your excursions, make sure to visit the Cabo Blanco Butterfly Garden and have yourself a silent dance party in the pack of butterflies flickering and fluttering to their own hushed pura vida.

Good for surfing, small towns, hikes, butterflies, jungle, chillin.'

Montezuma—Montezuma is a quaint bohemian town that warps time for many people. Named after the abundance of Montezuma oropendola, a chestnut and yellow painted bird, which call the area their home and make it a great location for bird watching. With a plethora of trees bearing fruit within the town, the low stress of Montezuma is one of those places people visit for a weekend and stay for years, (and surprisingly never age).

80- Horseback Riding to the Hidden Cascades of El Chorro

Playa Cocolito is another one of those hidden corners that Mother Nature made difficult to discover.

It is a hidden corner inaccessible by car or bus, the ideal way is to take nature's land rover (aka horseback) or trek it in. People venture out due to its seclusion and guaranteed lack of pasty tourists complaining over the bad wifi in the jungle. Once there, you'll find a very long beach with only a couple of shacks on it, and the few people in the area are probably heading towards the El Chorro waterfall. A small cove hides El Chorro waterfall, spouting turquoise waters off the cliff's edge and pouring into the ocean. It is one of those images that you have accidentally pinned to your Pinterest so many times because you get excited every time it pops up on your homepage. With the pristine white beaches and blending of blue-green waters, you wonder what Tom Hanks from Castaway was complaining about.

Good for diving, hiking, waterfalls, bird watching, and chillin.'

81- Ghost Hunting on Cabuya Island

Best kept secret

An island of lost souls, this floating cemetery lures the curiosity of locals and tourists alike toward the supernatural side of the tropics. Cabuya Island has been used as a cemetery for thousands of years; the native tribes buried their dead on the buoyant haven for centuries before the Spanish took over. It continues to be used as a burial ground—harboring centuries of ghosts, sadness and death. The natives have always believed that the island was laced with superstition, where spirits wander back and forth between portals connecting the living world and the unknown eternal home.

The locals play into the eeriness of the supernatural story. If a bad episode of 'Ghost Hunters' gets you going, I would suggest you take a night out with the locals when they walk out in the shallow waters to the nearby island, with lit candles to have a funeral or pay respects. From a distance, it appears as though floating auras are traveling back and forth from the mainland—pranking those trying to relax in the surrounding hills of Cabuya, Los Cedros, Delicias, and Montezuma.

A walkable shallow rocky path leads on to Cabuya Island from the mainland. Once you are there you can wander amongst the grave sites and walk on the burial grounds that contain thousands of years of decay and sorrow. If you choose to ignore the celestial stories and are more interested in the living it is a phenomenal snorkeling destination not many choose to risk venturing out to. Just hope that the iridescent fish that circle the island aren't phantoms themselves.

Good for ghost hunting, voodoo, witchcraft, pranks, and snorkeling.

82- Casting Spells in a Bioluminescence Tour

If you seek an adventure to experience a facet of our planet—a beautiful mutation and expression of our planet's immeasurable surprises, an awe-inspiring phenomenon—take a nighttime bioluminescent tour.

A little before dusk, you glide off the mainland into the mangroves that are slowly growing away from land. As you sail through this drowning forest the tour guide will explain that the mangroves produce the ideal habitat that the tiny luminous plankton thrive on. You will continue to navigate through the mangroves until you get to a spot where the trees start to taper off and you are on the precipice of the boundless ocean. He shuts off the motor and the waters will appear to be so clear that it is the perfect mirror for the stars silently peering down at you from the heavens. Then you realize that stars don't really cluster like that...tightly together and only reflected for a moment. The tour guide takes out a paddle and slices the water, making it bleed glitter. He begins jousting with the water as if battling a medieval dragon that was breathing sparkles. You won't believe your eyes. It looks like blueish, yellowish fireworks exploded in the water—a burst of blues and yellows expanding and then receding, until it finally returns to the customary cobalt blue.

The guide then hands you sticks to create your own magic while hanging off the side of the boat—trying to not fall into the water from excitement. Looking like wizards and witches casting spells into the water, you may swear you heard someone whisper, 'expecto patronum.' The guide turns on the boat and you venture further out into the ocean and watch the giant trail of plankton sparkle in the waters you left behind. Turning off the boat, your tour guide jumps into the water and you all follow quickly behind him. The feeling you have as you plunge in and open your eyes underwater, seeing your body illuminated with this aquatic alchemy, is impossible to describe. If I could live there forever, I would. I never wanted to stop swirling and dancing in this underwater aura illuminating the perimeter of my body. I was the first one to jump in and the last one to leave. And as we buzzed back to shore and I sat in the warmth in my dry towel, glad the motor was loud enough so the others couldn't hear the sounds of my sobbing.

83- The Hidden Black Sand Beach of Playa Zancudo

Are you sick of me describing all of these idyllic, pristine white beaches enclosed by coconut trees with chic travel adjectives? Then tell Costa Rica to stop being so damn gorgeous. All the beaches on Costa Rica truly are spectacular, but sometimes too much sun and white beach exposure can be harsh on your skin. And if you are like me (so pale that wearing shorts makes me afraid I'm contributing to global warming by reflecting the sun off my thighs) white sand beaches can feel more like you are camouflaging than tanning. Which brings me to the black sand beaches of Playa Zancudo.

This six mile stretch of sand is untouched by tourists (and even Ticos at that). It is a wonderful place to retreat into the mangroves and jungle surrounding it and enjoy true isolation from the world. Take your blanket out, lie on the ink stained sand and be the vanilla side of a black and white cookie.

Good for black sand beaches, isolation, and chillin.'

84- Tarcoles River Boat Crocodile Tour

There is a bridge on your way to Jaco that might be crowded with people leaning over and looking down. Sunbathing on the river banks of the Tarcoles River underneath, will be crocodiles of every size, looking back up at what they hope is breakfast, lunch and dinner. I suggest you take a guided tour if you want to have a staring contest with these crocs. The tour navigates through the dense mangrove canals and offers intimacy, not only with these prehistoric creatures, but with the other wildlife that calls this area their home.

Chapter 12: Jaco

After navigating so many isolated caves, beaches and islands, it might be nice to talk to someone new. Jaco is a more active area that will get you talking, dancing and surfing with all walks of life.

This lively beach was developed as a resort city originally planned by Charles Elwood Jaco. After inheriting the area he dreamed of turning it into a family resort community for everyone to enjoy, which it has successfully become today.

Jaco is a hot spot for surfing with a collection of surf shops and schools to take your surfing to the next level. The consistent gentle swell is perfect for those who are rusty or just starting to learn. There is a plethora of restaurants, bars, nightclubs and markets for you to enjoy as you spend a few days here.

85- Hablando Espanol

If you are getting tired of surfing and are more interested in talking to the locals, take a Spanish class. Spending an afternoon brushing up on your Spanish or taking a crash course. Most more-developed cities have tutors at every level that are willing to help you at any level of fluency. As someone who rarely knows when to stop talking, it was such a challenge to learn another language (especially as someone who dabbles in more ostentatious vernacular, learning how to stay basic phrases in Spanish was a rewarding (and humbling) experience).

Additionally, I have found that Spanish speakers are supportive when you try to speak to them in their broken mother tongue. One time, while looking out at a sunset, I turned to a local and said dramatically looking out into the distance "El atardecer es muy hermano" (the sunset is very brother) instead of HERMOSA (which means beautiful). Although most of my Spanish interactions end in "tranquillo gringa," everyone I spoke to was appreciative of my attempt. Unlike the French, though I could pontificate flawlessly in their language, they would generally reply with an unimpressed "Quoi?" You are able to see the area through the eyes of a local once you are able to communicate with them in their native language. Once you are in with the locals, they will tell you where to go to avoid all the gringos, and share information on where the good spots are.

Insider tip—if you have no idea what a local just said to you and don't want to look dumb, just say 'pura vida' and slow fade away.

86- Hablando Espanol con Ballar

Some alternative ways for practicing Spanish are to take a dance or yoga class offered in the language. This might be more mentally and physically taxing (justification for eating too many fried plantains), however, the movement and language connection will help you learn both faster. You are actively moving to the language and this hands on experience kills two birds with one stone.

87- Jaco Canopy Zipline Tour

If you are staying in the region for your trip and don't get an opportunity to zipline in Monteverde or Manuel Antonio, absolutely take advantage of the sights and soaring in Jaco. Apparently, the velocity of the ziplining tours in Jaco is higher and more extreme than your average adventure. So go for it, don't think about it—thinking ruins ziplining—and remember to breathe as you are flying above the treetops, waterfalls, and beaches, embodying the spirit of the birds.

88- Jaco Rainforest Aerial Tram

To be fair, ziplining is not for the faint of heart. However, an aerial tram tour will have you right at the same elevation, but at a slower pace, allowing you to take in the glory of the forest canopy around you. The tour teaches you about the diverse nature and wildlife, living right beneath your feet, as you comfortably glide above the peaks of the tops of the forest.

Good for shopping, nightlife, food & drink, beaches, hikes, surfing, snorkeling, diving, horseback riding, and ziplining.

89- Scarlet Macaws in Carara National Park

At the heels of the beach resorts is an vivaciously dense rain forest, teaming with regional wildlife unfolding into the surrounding mountain range.

Carara National Park has a small network of trails that treck through primary and secondary forest. Hiking through, you can take note of a wide variety of wildlife making their home in Carara—monkeys, leaf cutter ants, and a plethora of birds. In fact, this park is claimed to be one of the more ideal birding spots in the country ranging over 400 different species. Specifically, it has one of the largest populations of the rare scarlet macaw in Costa Rica. Take a look throughout the canopy and venture to Rainforest Adventures, an ecotourism adventure park where you can take an aerial tram through the canopy of the forest.

Good for birdwatching, aerial tram, canopy sights, ziplining, animals, and hiking.

90- Silence in Manuel Antonio

The Manuel Antonio National Park is the Costa Rica you dreamed of. If you can only go to one of the countless national parks, Manuel Antonio would be at the top of the list. Walking through Manuel Antonio is like exploring Jurassic Park, but sadly, with fewer dinosaurs. The far reaching park is nearly impossible to get through in one day, but there is no rush, no to-do list, no expectations. Just allow your feet to follow the pull of pura vida; she will show you what you need to see and let your brain take the backseat. There is a windy town build upon the hills outside of the park where you can bring a picnic and relax on the beach or nosh in the woods.

The park is connected by a series of wooden paths, and these veins of Manuel Antonio paths connect and circulate throughout the entire body of the park. The sound of your feet on wood at a pura vida pace will have you bumping into all the creatures of the park: sloths snuggled up in trees, anteaters vacuuming up their lunch and monkeys mistaking trash cans as playpens, jubilantly throwing the contents around. The paths have you rolling up and down the park's diverse topography. From the higher points, you will have a vantage that gives you a full frontal exposure of the park, including the rounded crescent shape the beach takes on, walled by large hills covered with tropical trees and the paragliders sailing the skies in the distance, easily mistaken for birds.

Although touristy, I was granted a few moments of serenity and total isolation—an intimate moment with just me and breathing pura vida forest—away from the

English and broken Spanish filling the park.

I wandered towards a circular wooden outlook on a small cliff to what I thought would be a waterfall (but only in the rainy season). Instead, it was a barren slide of rocks—but I was still able to inhale the silence and find beauty in the curves of the rocks, smoothly sculpted by the water for half of the year. I felt the stillness and slow movements of the forest—a leaf falling, a frog hopping, a bud blooming. It is a stillness that can make some uncomfortable. To those who are conditioned to never stop, like a shark—stillness means death. It's the kind of stillness that lets you feel your blood circulate, your cells reproduce and your heart beat. A stillness we are too often denied or have never met, constantly surrounded and overstimulated. That stillness was quickly snatched away by a blundering group of Australians, who loudly complained about there being no waterfall as they sipped beer out of paper bags and turned around on their heels. But, I still had my moment.

91- Canopy Safari Zip Line

The ziplining in Manuel Antonio is some of the oldest in the southern part of the country, so they know what they are doing. The tour includes propelling you above the canopy, giving you all-encompassing views down below, rappelling lines, suspension bridges and the stomach-lurching Tarzan swing. Ziplining will give you the adrenaline rush of a lifetime, like you are on a coffee high for the next few days.

92- White Water Rafting down Naranjo River

Nearby the park is the Naranjo River where you can tumble down these rapids on a whitewater rafting tours. There are several types of tours you can take depending on your thrill level. For the faint of heart and los ninos, there are tours that will usher you down an exciting—but not too exciting—channel before unfurling into the Pacific flatlands, transporting you to a calming flow and allowing you to observe the wild birds that live by the water's edge.

For a bit more of an adrenaline rush, you can rush down El Chorro, the jet. This extreme stretch has you going through twists and turns, as nine narrows turns and a tight squeeze through canyon walls, hug the raft.

Good for beaches, wildlife, hiking, walking,

stillness, ziplining, canopy walks, paragliding, beaches, white water rafting and chillin.'

Chapter 13: Uvita

There isn't as much of a central town in Uvita, and most of the action is hidden behind the beach, in hidden pockets that shade the locals from the blaring sun. It has great access to Marino Ballena National Park where you can get up close and personal with whale watching tours.

93- Become Clean in Cascada Verde

You can choose between the saltwater of the ocean or the freshwater of the secret waterfalls sprinkled around the area. On my first morning, I had trudged for an hour on a hilly dusty road, in punishing heat to reach a waterfall, in the kind of humidity that sticks to you. A thin layer of dust mixing with sweat began cementing itself onto my body, and I was ready to wash it off.

Once I arrived, there were already a few other people in the small, pristine pool at the base of the waterfall. I watched young boys with primate acrobatic skills climb up the slippery rocks and propel their bodies over the falls. And as I jumped into the cold water, I felt myself become clean again.

94- Walk the Whale's Tail at Marino Ballena National Park

The front yard of Uvita is Marino Ballena National Park. It is a mangrove forest that embroiders itself on the sand drawing a line between the jungle and sand. There is the traditional wildlife doing their thing in the ambient jungle, but the real star of the show is the tombolo Whale's Tail. "Tombolo translates to 'mound' and is a deposition landform in which an island is attached to the mainland by a narrow piece of land such as a spit or bar.

Once attached, the island is then known as a tied island.

This strange aquatic landform is a remarkable

natural barrier reef formed by the forces of two rivers on either side of the reef. The currents of these dual river systems sculpt and maintain the shape of a whale's tail when viewed from above. You can easily see and walk the formation at low tide or take a peek at it from the mountain range view above the town of Uvita-Bahía.

As incredible as this natural phenomenon is, the beach is rarely crowded, giving you plenty of silence in which to meditate on the bizarreness of the Whale's Tail. Contemplate how Mother Nature has more complexities and surprises than you realized. The magic of the whale's tail is that it disappears below the water, just like the real thing.

Good for kayaking, nature tours, surfing, stand up paddle boarding, snorkeling, and whale watching.

Chapter 14: Dominical

This intimate town is a bohemian mermaid paradise. There is a nice rotation of coffee shops, tropical bars and restaurants in which to spend an afternoon, plus access to numerous activities. If you want to keep it local, there is a charming strip of outside vendors that line the beach and are shaded by coconut trees. Every beach-lovers delight is being sold here from t-shirts, custom made jewelry, henna, crystals, sarongs, towels, handmade wooden items, musical instruments and even hammocks.

95- Flying and Paragliding

The desire to fly has been an ancient human desire. From the Wright Brothers to Leonardo Da Vinci, humans have always wanted to know what it is like to have wings. Fortunately, Dominical is one of the ideal places to explore this cornerstone desire of humanity. The illusion of this super power provides you with the ability to see everything at once. With the wind under your belly, you are able to soar above mountain ranges, the coast line, the whale's tale and the jungle, witnessing all of the glory of mother earth. At 1300 feet above the ocean, you will navigate slowly amongst the clouds. Land on the gentle sand along the coast line and jump right into the cool water to bring you back to earth.

96- Poisonous Frogs in Parque Reptilandia

Sometimes, it doesn't matter how many walks through the jungle you have taken, you might not get to see every wild thing up close and personal. If there are creatures that you want to see in a more contained environment, then visit Parque Reptilandia which has several enclosed spaces where you'll see reptiles native to the land. Expect to see plenty of snakes, tortoises, crocodiles, and lizards. There are even sections that have poisonous dart frogs! Reptile enthusiasts and the curious are welcome.

Good for kayaking, nature tour, paragliding,

surfing, stand up paddle boarding, snorkeling, whale watching, shopping, and horseback riding.

You have made it to the last leg of Costa Rica. The Osa Peninsula is by far the least explored, most mysterious, and filled with wonders for any intrepid traveler. Here is the land of giant marine mammals, gold mining, and unanswered archaeological questions.

97- Ojochal: The Gateway to Osa Peninsula

The door to Osa from is a muy tranquilo town of Ojochal located on the the Ballena Coast, before venturing into the dense jungles of Corcovado. The poorly paved roads are perfect for AV driving, an injection of adrenaline up the mountainside. You can venture up via AV through the jungle up to Cascada Pavón and cool yourself from the blazing Costa Rican sun. The dense forest is also a fantastic location for canopy tours or ziplining, where you can live an afternoon with the birds among the treetops. The proximity to the base of Marino Ballena National Park provides the opportunity for whale watching tours as well.

Good for AV tours, bird watching, hiking, waterfalls, ziplining, canopy tours, and whale watching.

Chapter 15: Caño Island

If you are in the Drake Bay area, visiting Cano Island is a must. This unpretentious island offers way more than one would expect. First it is one of the most unique scuba diving and snorkeling locations in Costa Rica—ranging from macro to micro aquatic life. On the larger end, this spot gives opportunity to white tip sharks, bull sharks, dolphins, manta rays, jumping mobula rays, or maybe if you are lucky, a whale shark. On the smaller end of life, you might think you are discovering a new form of giant fish in the distance, but up close you will realize that it is just a ginormous school of little guys! Divers frequently encounter schools of vibrant fish scaling in the hundreds in these crystal clear waters.

98- Diving in the Devil's Rock

El Bajo del Diablo (or 'Devil's Rock') is a prime spot to see the big and little fish alike. This location is found a little over a mile off the island's shore. Weave in and out of the mountainous underwater rock pyramids that stretch from the ocean floor, forming what looks like a miniature underwater mountain range.

99- Shark Tank

Do you live every week like it's Shark Week? The Shark Cave, Cueva del Tiburón, as the locals call it, is home to several white tip sharks, and adventurers are expected to witness a handful of these sharks sleeping in the mouth of the cave. Watching these carnivorous fish peacefully recuperate does not make the situation less unsettling, if anything it feels almost like a trap.

Due to park regulations, divers cannot enter the cave, but is that really so surprising? The cave is surrounded and hedged by iridescent coral gardens, adding a magical touch to the cave.

100- The Coral Gardens

The Coral Gardens will make you feel like you are walking through an embellished English garden. The budding and blossoming with aquatic landscape is layered with a rainbow of hard coral. This is a more tranquil option than the heart racing dives of El Diablo and the Shark Cave. Float along the vast variety of tropical fish such as the damselfish, the parrotfish, the butterflyfish, the porcupine fish, the goby, and perhaps even an octopus! The simple elegance of this underwater oasis will have you itching to paint the scenery and ask for tea.

101- Mysterious Spheres of Caño Island

Let's leave our last adventure on a real mystery. The second, and more magical aspect of the Cano Islands are the mythical and mysterious spheres of a lost ancient indigenous tribe.

Sitio Arqueológico Finca 6 is a rare archeological site and regionally referred to as Las Bolas (translation: The Balls). It is believed that the spheres were created by the extinct Diquís culture, a pre-Columbian tribe. Some 300 of these spheres were found on the Cano

Island and their mainland neighbor the Diquís Delta. These perfectly (and I mean perfectly) rounded spheres are made from numerous stones, sculpted out of sandstone, limestone, gabbro and granodiorite from the nearby Costeña coastal range. The Diquis used stone tools also made by hand and transported them to the island!

Wait! What does this mean?! Well we actually don't know and their true function remains a mystery. The spheres were dug up on what might have been a burial ground or trading post for the mysterious pre-Columbian indigenous culture. However, their main purpose is still cloudy. One correlation found is them being buried with individual tribesmen. The bigger the sphere, the more powerful the individual, and several have been found with what are assumed to be chiefs. Other theories suggest that since several of the spheres are found in a formation, assuming an intentional alignment, or were discovered in groups; they may symbolize some celestial phenomena or serve a purpose as solar calendars. The grandest of them all weighs 24 tons. If you don't get a chance to see them in their original state, the Natural Museum in San Jose has a few on display in their garden. The Diquís spheres are protected by UNESCO's World

Heritage Sites.

Good for snorkeling, diving, swimming, mysteries.

Final Words

Although we did just go through an impressive list of 101 adventures, activities and sights to participate in, we have just skimmed the surface. This country offers so much in the tiny space it occupies, offering immersion and discovery with our earth on every level: land, sea and sky. Here, you are able to live out every superpower humans have ached for since we realized we could not fly like birds or breathe underwater.

These opportunities will expand and challenge your understanding of the world-learn what it is like to soar through the air, warm your body near geothermal energies, or delve into the depths of our oceans. Not many places provide such a wide range of ways to experience your body in other elements. Whether you are going for a week or end up never returning (don't worry, plenty of people "get lost in the rainforest" and "never return") remember to embody the lessons that pura vida taught you.

This is a guide book, not a to do list. Bring out your inner explorer and push yourself to step off the main trail and find unity with the land that you occupy.

Bonus: the Secret for Cheap Flights

Did you know there are travelers who never pay for flights? Or when they pay, they pay very little.

Some are people who travel full time. Some are people with normal jobs. Some are moms and dads, others are single travelers.

They're the same as everyone else - with one big exception:

They don't pay for flights. They can travel anywhere they want, whenever they want.

So before you travel, make sure you know the 3 tips to get the cheapest flights possible.

There are 3 ways you can get cheap flights.

1) Use Error Fares

2) Use Throwaway Tickets

3) Get (Almost) Free Flights

1. Look for Error Fares

Error fares are cheap plane tickets that the airlines put up online by mistake. You can find these on websites like SecretFlying.com or AirfareWatchdog.com.

These flights can be as much as 50% below what you'd normally pay. That said, they only leave from certain destinations and only go to certain places.

2. Use Throwaway Tickets

Did you know it's sometimes cheaper to book a LONGER flight.. and throw away the second portion?

Example: Instead of booking New York to Texas, it might be cheaper to book a ticket from New York to

Los Angeles, with a layover in Texas.

Just get off at the layover and discard the 2nd leg of the flight.

3. The Secret to book $1,000 flights for just $20 or less. (MOST IMPORANT)

This strategy is the easiest and most effective of the three. By using a few tricks to earn frequent flyer miles really quickly (without being a frequent flyer,) you can basically get free flights over and over and over.

As a small token of my appreciation for you reading this book, I have a FREE gift for you showing this Secret to book $1,000 flights for just $20 or less.

Check out the video showing you how on my website at: www.JamesHallTravel.com/TravelHack

I hope that it would help you save money on your flight tickets like I did, so you can travel more and enjoy what life has to offer!

Enjoy!

James Hall

Thanks for reading! If you like the book, please write a short review on Amazon with your thoughts. Also, if you like this book, please let others know, in order to share the awesomeness of Italy!

Still interested in my other travel books?

I have many more to come. I intend to write about all the places that I traveled to.

Connect with me on my website at www.JamesHallTravel.com, or check out my Amazon Author Page for my new books: https://www.amazon.com/James-Hall/e/B01M5K2N8F.

James Hall

Thailand

ULTIMATE TRAVEL GUIDE TO THE BEST OF THAILAND

JAMES HALL

101+ THINGS You Must Do In RETIREMENT

ULTIMATE GUIDE TO AN AWESOME LIFE AFTER WORK

JAMES HALL

James Hall

101 AWESOME THINGS YOU MUST DO IN JAPAN

JAMES HALL

Printed in Great Britain
by Amazon